H.M.S.
WELLINGTON

ONE SHIP'S WAR

H.M.S. WELLINGTON

ONE SHIP'S WAR

G.J. WILLIAMS

Published 1992 by
The Self Publishing Association Ltd,
Units 7/10, Hanley Workshops,
Hanley Road, Hanley Swan,
Worcs.

A MEMBER OF

in conjunction with
G.J. WILLIAMS

British Library Cataloguing in Publication Data
A catalogue record for this book is available from the British Library

ISBN 1 85421 166 8

Designed and Produced by Images Design and Print Ltd.
Printed and Bound in Great Britain by Hartnolls, Cornwall.

Dedication

For all the help and encouragement from Grace.

All my love and thanks.

PROLOGUE

Just below Waterloo Bridge, on the River Thames in London, what remains of a wartime Sloop slumbers quietly at her mooring in retirement. She is listed in the guide books as *The Wellington*. Some of them even pay her the compliment of saying HMS *Wellington*.

Occasionally, from one of the boats filled with tourists that motor by along the river, someone will throw her a silent kiss, while the guide may perhaps comment, "We are passing the *Wellington*."

It has been recorded that two ladies drop flowers into the river every year from a boat as they pass her, and elderly gentlemen in taxis will lift their hats as they drive by. The drivers of coaches coming into the Capital have been asked to detour a little, so that some of the older passengers can catch a glimpse of what was once a warship. She belongs now to The Honourable Company of Master Mariners.

Historians will say that she had an undistinguished war record, but her wartime crew will hardly agree with that, but you judge for yourself as you read on.

Who am I? I was just one of her wartime crew. She brought me, and hundreds like me, safely home from the wilderness of the North Atlantic in the dark days of the early 1940s.

She bore a charmed life, helped no doubt by the rabbit's foot kept in the starboard lifebelt locker. It was this ship, her crew, and that rabbit's foot that gave those so called historians the freedom to say she had an undistinguished war, but then, none of them had the chance to sail with her.

If you know where to look, you can still see the scars of some of the near misses she suffered, but I will tell you about these as we go along. Some of the events may not be in sequence, but they did happen, and some of the girls' names have been changed for obvious reasons. They will be older now, with daughters of their own, but they will recognise themselves, and I hope they will forgive me.

Chapter One

In 1939 New Entry Class 178 was not very far off completing their training at HMS *Drake*, which was the Naval Barracks at Devonport, Plymouth. On the playing fields, we were practising for the field gun competition which is now a big part of the Royal Tournament at Earls Court in London. On that fateful Sunday morning, when our Prime Minister declared war on Germany, the barracks shook under the roar of cheers that greeted his words.

Six long months of training was behind us. Our parade ground drill was a joy to see, or so we thought. We had been shouted at, threatened, chased, insulted. In our white belts and gaiters, and burnished steel bayonets fixed to our rifles, we were deemed fit at last to march with precision across the parade ground, while the Marine Band belted out *Hearts of Oak*. If it was wet, then we would do it in the huge drill shed, where the noise and shouts sounded much worse.

At Sunday Morning Divisions, we were there, in the forefront. Only the Training Division could demonstrate, fresh from the classrooms, what the Royal Navy should look like while on parade.

If your bayonet comes off and sticks in your head, we were told, leave it! Keep going through the motions.

Such was Naval discipline drummed into us that once, in the silence of a prayer, the Gunnery Officer, standing in front of his Training Division platoon in the drill shed, slowly shifted his weight to his right leg, and lifted his highly polished black leather gaitered left leg, and loudly farted.

Hymn books dropped all over the drill shed, but Class 178, who got the full blast of it, never faltered.

Beyond the parade ground, and across the road in the dockyard, the massive bulk of a refitting battleship, the *Valiant*, loomed over the dividing fences. We could see her big fifteen-inch guns being delivered by rail.

The Royal Naval Barracks, Devonport, in 1939.

"That's where we will be going," guessed Tom. "To commission her will take a hundred of our classes." He was probably right. But in the meantime, we still had a lot to learn.

Our instructor was a proud Scotsman, Leading Seaman Jock Coats, and we had to call him Sir. He took us from nervous young civilians marching into Barracks from the train at Keyham while still dressed in civilian clothes, to experts on the parade ground that were a joy to watch.

Foam used to gather around his mouth as he shouted at us, and we blushed like girls as he showed us how to bath, or shower, in the basement of Exmouth Block.

"Pull the skin back," he instructed us. "Wash the cheese out. Our girls are too precious to be infected by you lot!"

We had never thought about infecting any of our girls, but we would think about it from now on.

From the parade ground and the anti gas school, through the gunnery school, and to sea in a destroyer to practise real gunfire with seasickness thrown in for good measure. Then to seamanship classes, and sailing off Drakes Island in a cutter, dodging *Torpoint Ferry* while rowing in a whaler, to wrestling with the steering wheel of our toy warship being thrown around by small electric motors, while our Jock passed steering orders to us from a glassed off compartment at the side of the classroom.

Training Division had to come to and end sometime, and our passing out parade was in wartime. There were no cheering families, just brass bands and precision marching, and Leading Seaman Jock Coats stood proudly on the sidelines as we marched out of his life on to the books of the drafting office.

Just as Tom had predicted, many of those classes from Training Division were marched off to form part of the crew of the battleship HMS *Valiant*. A few joined the destroyer *Punjabi*, and sixteen of us had orders to report to something called the *Wellington*.

Embarkation leave: we were sent off home for seven days. After all, *Wellington* sounded as if it was somewhere in New Zealand. Heaven alone knew when we would see home again. There was a tearful farewell as I left mother and home in the Rhondda Valley for my first appointment to HMS *Wellington*.

Not until we arrived back at Cardiff railway station from Plymouth did we have any idea where we were going. Navy trucks collected us at the station and delivered us to a dry dock where it seemed a ship was being torn apart.

She was dwarfed by the big dry dock she was sitting in. She was dirty and seemed to be in pieces. A bearded Petty Officer in greasy overalls, looking positively dangerous, glared up at us as we lined the dock wall.

Hopefully, it might be the wrong ship, but seeing her name in large, brass letters on the bulkhead near the gangway soon put paid to that. We were eighteen, fresh from the white belts and gaiters of Training Division, in smart uniforms that had never felt a spot of sea water.

After a while, someone reluctantly came to talk to us, and we were shown to our messes, allocated a locker for our kit, and told where we could sling our hammocks.

A sailor in dirty overalls made us a cup of tea in a pot the size of a small dustbin. Looking at us over the rim of his cup, and hiding behind the two stripes on his arm that we had not yet learned to deal with, he said, "That is the last time I shall make you lot a wet of tea. From now on, you will make it for me."

The *Wellington*, we were informed, was a new ship, built only five years before. She had been paying courtesy calls on the islands around New Zealand at the outbreak of war, and had been ordered home immediately. Here in Bute Dock, she was being hastily prepared for war. Her saluting guns were being ripped out, and depth charge rails and throwers were being fitted on her quarterdeck.

She had two hefty 4.7 inch guns in well protected turrets, one forward, and one aft, and a three inch high angle gun on B deck as defence against aircraft.

Mother was startled and delighted to have her wandering boy home again so soon after sending him off to war. Not Sally though, who three days before had bid her sailor boy a tearful goodbye at the local railway station, and who was now proudly parading through Main Street on the arm of an airman from the nearby RAF Station. It is feared that Naval and RAF combined operations was at a low ebb before HMS *Wellington* was ready at last for sea.

The dockyard had done well with the ship. There were more watertight compartments, strengthened deck supports for the guns, larger storage for ammunition, and submarine detection equipment. With her camouflage, she looked like a zebra hiding behind a tree. All around her quarterdeck, fittings had been installed to hold depth charges to supply two dropping rails aft, and a thrower on each side. The depth charges from the rails could be released by levers up on the bridge, but the throwers could only be fired by someone pulling out the firing pin.

By mid January 1940, the *Wellington* was ready for sea. Cranes lifted out the welding sets and buckets of tools. She had been moved out of the dry dock and was now waiting alongside the wall. All day we had loaded stores and ammunition, and several lorry loads of depth charges had been rolled aboard and stowed around the quarterdeck.

By tea time it was raining, and a cold wind was coming in from the Bristol Channel. The weather forecast gave it as strong to gale southwesterly. The *Wellington* eased away from the wall, and edged through a narrow channel that led to the open sea. I shrivel with humiliation even now as I remember the harbour master standing on the dock side, with a big, fat belly, shouting up at me, "Get a fender down here!"

I ran and got a fender, a real heavy one, and tried to lower it down between the ships' side and the dock wall she was scraping against. Only the rope wasn't long enough for the fender to reach the place where it was wanted.

I smiled sweetly at that fat harbour master as he spat in the water, and tried not to notice the new paintwork being scraped off as the ship rubbed against the wall, while a useless fender swung daintily half way up her side.

In spite of any hindrance from me, she cleared the harbour

and headed out into the Bristol Channel, ready for war.

She might have been. But her crew certainly wasn't.

My first duty as soon as we were clear of the harbour was masthead lookout. Oh, I had climbed masts before in Training Division times without number, but they hadn't moved like this one was. If the *Wellington* seemed small in dock to us when we first saw her, it seemed to me now that her mast reached right up to the clouds. I edged upwards, one step at a time. Whenever I dared to look down to see how far I had come, all I could see were white faces stareing up at me.

The ladder I was climbing was at the back of the mast, but the crow's nest was at the front; to reach it I had to climb up over the yard arm. When I finally reached safety, it didn't help in the least to think that I had to go through it all again in order to get down.

There was a small seat in there, and a metal box that held a telephone. I picked the phone up to look at it, and a voice said, "Yes?" I looked over the edge, a Signalman down on the bridge was holding a phone and looking up at me. I waved faintly, and put it back. At least, now I knew what it was for. While sitting on that seat no one on the ship could see you.

After a while, I felt the mast beginning to shake in a different kind of way, and looked down to see another of my Training Division class clinging to the ladder down there at the bottom. He never got beyond ten steps before going back down again.

Shortly after, my phone howled, and I looked over at the bridge and shouted, "What?"

Somebody shook a fist at me, and brandished a phone. Remembering, I shamefaced picked it up.

"Come on down", a voice said. Trembling, I crawled over that yard arm, and clung for dear life to the ladder as I let myself down. My first lookout duty was accomplished.

It was getting dark, and a warm smell of cooking was coming from the ventilators and hatches, but a head wind was pushing the sea into the arms of the Bristol Channel, and this strange creature we had been sent to crew seemed to be intent on shaking the dust of Cardiff from her many nooks and crannies. To us new members it seemed she was trying to shake us off as well. If anything was loose, she moved it. If you forgot to close and fasten a locker door, she emptied it. And if you put down a bucket of dirty water to reach for something, it was hard luck, mate, she tipped it.

Well before Hartland Point, her new crew were suffering. We had all done our boatwork at Saltash, and done our gunnery work on a destroyer. But this was different, this was for real. There was no fun or excitement about this.

It was pitch black by now, with no welcoming lights from the land or from other ships. Occasionally, there would be a flash of white froth as the crest of a wave sped by, and she would lean over towards it as if whispering a secret as it washed her side.

At 1800, or at four bells in the first dog watch, we were relieved by the watch below, and would be off duty now until 2000, or eight bells, though it would be a long time before bells would mean anything to us half drowned, half starved, and half dead, supposed to be sailors.

Hungry we might be, but the way that messdeck was leaping about put paid to any of us eating; nor did we find any humour in the way the plates were sliding about on the table. There was no sympathy from the older men, or loving hands to mop our brows. Whether we had eaten or not, we were still expected to wash the dishes and put them safely away.

"And that means making sure the locker door is bloody well fastened," warned one of our Stripey's. "If any of our cups get spilled out and smashed you'll be the ones who'll go without."

There was always plenty of boiling water in the galley. A coal fire that never went out kept it cosy and warm, and a capped ventilator on the deck above it spilled out warm air just aft of the bridge, but we hadn't learnt about that yet.

At sea, all through the night, there was a large pan, called a kettle, simmering on the galley range, full of almost black cocoa. We called it cae. I never saw that kettle empty, as it was always being topped up with boiling water from the taps on each side of the range. If the mixture looked a bit weak, we would drop in a few more blocks of what looked like chocolate to thicken it up a bit.

It took a lot of tinned milk to lighten a cup of that mixture. With men coming and going all through the night, milk and sugar were in short supply.

There was a sink there too, in the corner of the galley. It was the nearest sink to our messdecks. Our Petty Officer cook, known to all of us as Chef, was usually there in the galley. He made bread almost every day and cooked whatever we brought him from the messes. He kept that galley sparkling. We never saw him tip anything, or spill hot fat, even when the *Wellington* was in her worst mood.

We used to empty our washing up water down that sink, even when Chef was watching, as no power on earth would have taken us up onto that black and sea washed deck from the well lighted and cosy messdeck.

By 2000, the starboard watch of so called seamen, supposedly fed, warmed and dried, were ready to take over the watch on deck again. Thank heavens for the Stripeys, the men with one, two, or three stripes on their arms, signifying years of service. They cajoled, guided and threatened during that first night as the *Wellington* thumped her way from Cardiff, round Hartland Point, on to Land's End, and turned into the English Channel bound for our home port of Plymouth.

The Leading Seaman of the Watch detailed us for the lookout points. For the first half hour I found myself on the port side of the bridge, peering through a magnificent pair of binoculars.

After a while, getting brave and experienced, I really began to look. To my surprise, I saw a small ship some way off going the same way we were.

Remembering the wooden model we had learnt to steer and

report on from our Training Division days that now seemed so long ago, I squeaked, "Vessel bearing red eight oh, Sir!"

"Wot!" Consternation on the bridge. Captain, First Lieutenant, Officer of the Watch, and Signalman were at once all lined up along the bridge rail like punters on Derby Day.

"I can't see anything", growled someone.

"Oh, Gawd!" I silently prayed. "Not water on my glasses".

But no, there she was. I could see her.

At that moment, revelling in her freedom, the *Wellington* seemed to slip sideways, as if trying to chuck us off. From below came an almighty crash of smashing dishes as some unfastened locker opened. Her propellers came out of the water, and she shook herself, as if she was laughing. It was a rotten trick that she had, and she would perform it often. The real purpose of it was to make sure that any dishes still left in those open lockers would be shaken out.

Still no one on the bridge could see my ship, but I could. Finally, the First Lieutenant put his binoculars on top of mine, and after a while, to my overwhelming relief, announced, "I've got her".

From then on my fate was sealed. If there was anything missing, anything that was wanting to be found, then keen eyed Muggins was sent for, and whether on or off watch, would be dispatched to the crow's nest. It wasn't that I had keener eyes than anyone else. It was just that there was something to see when I happened to be looking.

From the bridge, it was back to the turret of B gun overlooking the quarterdeck, to join the rest of the Watch on deck who were not on lookout duty, or being sick. There was no heating in any of the turrets, they were dark, cold, and draughty, and every now and again the damned ship would heave a few buckets of seawater over them that would find its way through openings to drip all over us.

Someone coming off lookout duty on the bridge mentioned

that it was nice and warm near the ventilator over the galley, so it hadn't taken us long to find where the warm spots were. But there was too much water splashing about there to be safe to linger long. Besides, the smell of food was too strong for seasick stomachs to bear.

From the darkness of the turret, I voiced what was in most of our minds.

"Someone must be steering this bitch. Who would that be?" and from one of the only two seats in the turret came our Leading Seaman's voice, "It'll be you soon. Take over from Smithy in ten minutes". I fervently wished I had kept my mouth shut.

To reach the wheelhouse, we had been told not to use the door leading into the Captains flat from the boat deck while the ship was at sea. On a rough night, water could get in and rush down onto the messdeck below, where hammocks would be slung and men sleeping. We were to use the ladder to the signal deck, and go in by one of the wheelhouse doors on each side of it.

I stood in the dark on that signal deck wondering should I knock on the wheelhouse door and hope that someone would tell me to come in. Or should I just open the door and walk in. There were people above me on the bridge; I could hear them, although I couldn't see them. Below and in front of me were her bows, and bursts of white spray were flying back from her sharp end. Occasionally, she seemed to dip her head into the waves and fling back a mass of white water that would cover her anchor cables and winch and smash into her breakwater before crashing into A gun turret. It was no place for anyone to be moving about down there.

Ah well, she was my ship. I had a right to go anywhere I wanted. There was a door right here beside me. Why walk round to the other side? I would be faced with the same problem if I went round there. What the hell! Why knock? I lived here. I just opened the door.

The wrong one, of course. On the weather side. It flew open

with a crash, and I shot in still holding onto the doorknob. Papers went flying, and even the poor sod on the wheel leapt for safety. It took all of my strength to get that door shut, and no one helped. Everyone in there shouted, "Shut that bloody door!"

After the wet blackness of the gun turret the wheelhouse looked quite comfortable. There was a shielded light over a desk, a chair and a stool.The doors were polished wood. The engine-room telegraphs and binnacle were of well polished brass and had dim lights in them. The compass swung in its gimbals with her every movement, and the giro compass glared with a green light at face level and ticked loudly like an unoiled clock. The black metal balls of the compass adjusters looked like the heads of two wise men watching our every move.

"One eight seven", Smithy told me, nodding at the giro. "She's carrying above five degrees of port wheel, and she's on two, two-seven revs." He moved sideways for me to take over, and joined the Petty Officer of the Watch sitting on the desk.

Smithy was a two badge able seaman. He was the Quartermaster of this watch, and knew what he was about. There were never enough men like him on any ship. For now, I was his temporary helmsman.

Training Division had well prepared us for this. I knew what to do and how to do it, but still felt short of breath as I grasped that wheel. The numbers on the giro were never still. You could feel the sea punching her in the face, and see the effect each of these blows were having by the way the giro reacted to them; like a pretty girl smacking an over eager male in the face and he turning aside. The green numbers would run swiftly away from the alloted one-eight-seven, accompanied by an agitated clicking. A turn of the wheel would stop the numbers running and silence the clicking, and like a gentleman turning to face his lady again, the numbers would run back. But not too fast, or they would run on the other way.

It took a while, and sweat bearded the down on my as yet unshaven upper lip. But before my hour was up HMS *Wellington* was doing more or less what I wanted her to do. She had a mind of her own, but I felt equal to her. I would never again be afraid to take that wheel. At age eighteen, I felt this was one female I was going to enjoy arguing with.

With an almighty crash, the weather side door burst open, and another of my training class fell in. I joined in with all the others as they shouted, "Shut that bloody door."

Feeling twelve feet tall, and trying not to see the Petty Officer watching, I handed over the helmsman duty to him. "One-eight-seven", I told him, nodding at the green giro, "and she's carrying a shade over five degrees of Port wheel."

"Right", muttered Chopper uncomfortably as he took the wheel from me, handling it as if it was a female breast. Feeling superior, I reached for the doorknob.

"What about our speed?" demanded Smithy from his seat on the desk. "Tell him what speed we're doing."

"Oh." I glanced at the revolution counter. "Two, two-seven revs." I doubt if Chopper heard me. He wouldn't have heard me if I had told him there was a naked woman standing behind him. He was standing there transfixed, staring at the giro, and it was starting to run.

I got the hell out of there just as a protesting voice from the bridge above bellowed through the voice pipe. "Who's on the wheel?"

And went out through the wrong flaming door again.

At midnight, the starboard watch came on duty, and the watch that I was a part of could stand down. Damp and cold, and ill with sea sickness, I was able to climb at last into my hammock for blissful oblivion. But only for four hours. At 0400 the port watch would take over again.

Lying there, with every bone aching from constantly trying to keep your balance, it was bliss to feel your hammock doing the balancing for you. I could hear the sea smashing into the ships side near to where I lay and the sound of rushing water on the deck above my head. There were all kinds of creaks and rattles going on, and the sound of things moving and sliding as the ship rolled.

For a while, fear gripped me. I was an active service rating; I hadn't been called up; I had been stupid enough to volunteer, and had been three quarters of the way through training before war had been declared. People being called up now would only have a couple of weeks training before being sent to sea, compared to ours of nearly a year.

"Oh, mother. What have I done?" She must have heard me, and I felt her touch my face. I kissed her hand, and opened my eyes as I felt it recoil. I was staring down straight at Fred, another of my training class. He was rubbing his hand as if it burnt.

"What the hell d'you want?"

"Quarter to four", he tells me. "You've just got time for a cup of cae (cocoa). You'll want your oilskins, its wet up top."

I hardly needed him to tell me that; I could hear the water rushing along the deck just above my head.

In the galley, the kettle was only half full. Somebody topped it up with boiling water and dropped in another block. There was no milk or sugar left. Still, it was hot.

Climbing the ladder from the port passage just aft of the galley brought you out onto the boat deck, and it was a sight that I would never get used to. You were out on the open deck with no lights except what nature provided. You would stop there for a moment, holding on to anything handy, letting your eyes get used to the darkness, and soon you would see the white tops of the waves passing along her sides, and the white wake stretching away into the distance behind. The thicker the clouds, and the darker it became, the more clearly would you see the phosphorescent flecks in the passing waves and in the water being churned up by her screws.

The whine from her turbines was very noticeable here. It was a comforting, exhilarating sound, and you could feel the vibration and the rumble of her machinery, like the life blood pulsing around something alive. From Barry Roads, past Foreland, round Hartland Point with the wind in her teeth, to Land's End, then into the English Channel with the wind feeling easier as she ran with it, until the welcoming sight of the Eddystone came into view ahead.

Not until we were rounding Drakes Island in Plymouth Sound did she stop her antics, and Torpoint Ferry had a near miss as we took her up to Devonport. At last she was quiet alongside the wall, and the starving remnants of Class 178 could think of food again.

Seasickness vanished like magic. Most of us had girl-friends ashore who wouldn't be expecting to see us again for a while. There would be egg and chips in Aggie Westons, which was our affectionate name for the Royal Sailors Rests, and perhaps a fight with the Bootnecks, as we called the Marines.

It would be too cold to go bathing, or swim for the raft off the Hoe. But it was Plymouth. We were home.

I bought my first camera there during that first day ashore, a Box Brownie. It would take many pictures of the coming war at sea, but none of us knew anything about that yet.

Chapter Two

When we left Plymouth a few days later we had no idea where we were going. Classed as a sloop, the *Wellington* was bigger than a corvette, but not as big, or as fast, as a destroyer. She had more space for provisions and fuel than a destroyer, so could stay at sea longer. The Captain's accommodation on the boat deck below the wheelhouse was quite luxurious compared to everyone else's. Perhaps for this reason, her Captain was usually of Commander rank, whereas the Captain of a destroyer would be a Lieutenant Commander. After ten days at sea, a destroyer would be suffering, but a sloop could plod along quite happily for three weeks or more. She made her own fresh water, and there was a tank of iced drinking water on the stoker's mess deck.

There was a small compartment forward of the galley with the grand name of NAAFI Canteen that seemed able to stock everything we required from chocolate to cigarettes, sausages to bacon. She was allowed to carry a Canteen Manager as well, but he went to action stations like the rest of us.

With memories of the last rough ride she had given us, and of how we had suffered from it, it was not all sweetness and light as we eased her away from the wall and pointed her towards Plymouth Sound. Torpoint Ferry seemed to remember her and appeared to scuttle out of the way as we passed. Increasing speed as soon as we left the shelter of the Breakwater, we turned down Channel, heading for Falmouth.

Assembling there was the first convoy of ships that we had ever seen. Over thirty of them were milling around, squeezing into pre-arranged positions, hooting angrily at each other and belching smoke. Before dark, this mass of shipping, strung out over five miles of sea, was on the move. In the lead, like Christ leading his flock across the desert, was the *Wellington*.

There was not another warship in sight. We looked at each other uncomfortably, the same unspoken thought in everyone's mind. Someone seemed to have more faith in us than we did ourselves. Or did they know something that we didn't?

With nothing in front of us except America, we moved out into the vastness of the Atlantic Ocean with the convoy strung out behind us in five lines. The leading ship in the middle line was usually the biggest and fastest, so that he could get away quicker, we joked. The Commodore of the convoy would be aboard that one, along with his Signal Staff.

It was a hairy first night as HMS *Wellington* zig-zagged across the track of the oncoming ships. We had to learn fast about the perils of convoying, but so too, did the ships in the convoy. None of them knew anything about station keeping. Or about darkening ship.

Angry toots could be heard as faster ships overtook slower ships. One of them had his steaming lights on just as if he was on a pre-war cruise, and there were portholes open blasting out lights on most of them.

It was not much use us tip-toeing through the menace ahead if the gang behind was doing a Rumba. After much cussing and pointing, the *Wellington* abandoned her role as head scout and steamed down between the lines of ships, using her loud hailer to pointedly tell each of them what lights she was showing.

By the time the middle watch took over at midnight, it was hard to locate the convoy astern. Thirty ships were now following my leader, and keeping a wary eye on others each side of them.

The overall speed of this mass of shipping had to be the speed of the slowest vessel, usually between seven and eight knots. Everybody these days could do eight knots, we thought, and that was the declared speed of the convoy. So it would be reasonable to expect that every ship would be in its correct position when daylight came again and we could see them.

No fear! There were gaps in the lines and tell-tale smoke from over the horizon astern. There was nothing for it except to have a few words with the Commodore over a signal lamp. A flurry of flags would be hoisted on her mast, and when each ship in the convoy had read the signal and hoisted his answering pennant, which indicated he knew what it meant, down it would come; with luck and many crossed fingers, each ship should obey.

It was astonishing to see all that mass of shipping turning together. One or two perhaps wouldn't get it right, and we would grin as we saw them hurrying to catch up with the turn. Within minutes, they were all heading back the way they had come, and in an hour or so those distant puffs of smoke would be solid ships again taking up their positions once more.

Convoy number one for us was getting in some great practise that would stand those Captains in good stead for the horror that was to come in the years ahead.

The *Wellington* was the only escort that convoy had. As dawn was judged to be the most dangerous time, the ship went to action stations well before daylight. Everyone aboard was involved in that, which was hard luck on those who had completed the middle watch and had only just got turned in. All watertight doors and hatches would be closed and screwed down. Those people below would be effectively sealed down there, and those above unable to move below.

After an hour or so, when it became possible to see all round, and there was nothing in sight that shouldn't have been, life would return to the usual routine, the duty watch would take over, and the off duty crew would turn in again, if only for an hour.

Breakfast on the *Wellington* was something that seldom happened. After disturbed nights, everyone slept on for as long as possible, just coming awake in time for a quick wash and a cup of tea before starting work.

There was plenty of work to be done during the day. Tables and mess decks would be scrubbed white, cutlery and brasswork polished. Any accidents that might have occurred during the night, like flour, or sugar falling out of unfastened lockers, or china smashed, would be cleared up. Up on deck, hosepipes would be sluicing sea water, while crew members with long handled scrubbing brushes would bring the deck up snowy white.

There was always rust patches that had to be wire brushed clean, then red leaded, and finally painted grey.

The afternoons were quiet periods, when everyone not on watch would try and catch up on lost sleep.

The pinging of her asdics never stopped, night or day, and at first could be heard all around the bridge area, but after two days the loud speaker was switched off, much to the relief of everyone. Now, only the asdic rating in a small cabin at the back of the bridge could hear it through his headphones.

All asdic ratings were insane; we all believed that, and after listening to that noise all watch, who wouldn't be? They played up to this by walking about with tongues hanging out, or fingers sticking in their ears. They couldn't fool our Petty Officers though: when there was work to be done they had to do their share, no matter how far out their tongues were hanging.

Whenever the asdic made contact it was a tense period while it was being investigated. The Officer of the Watch would join the rating on the headphones before calling the Captain to the bridge. The ship would turn away from her course towards the echo, and she would slow down, warily probing the danger. The loudspeaker would be switched on, and we would all listen as length, speed, depth would be measured. A whale, or a shoal of fish could give a good echo. A whale would soon blow, and we would see it, but a shoal of fish could lead you a merry dance.

After about five days it was assumed the worst danger was now behind us. The convoy could be dispersed, and the ships could go on their way independently. Flag signals were hoisted aloft and, like a bus load of children on a Sunday school outing, our charges broke ranks. With funnels belching smoke as they opened throttles they forged away from us. There were hoots of farewell, and people lining the guard rails waved towels and shirts to us and shouted good luck as they went by.

Only the three persistent stragglers that we had to go back for every morning seemed reluctant to leave. They seemed to have slowed down even more than usual. Perhaps they thought the race was over, there was no need to hurry any more.

A gun drill on HMS Wellington

Soon, the *Wellington* had the ocean to herself. Increasing to fourteen knots, she turned northwards and, after a few hours in a wicked mood and after due warning to her ships company, she slowed and went to action stations. For an hour, we threw her about and ended with three rounds from each of those 4.7s, just to see what they sounded like, and then a few from the 3 inch for good measure. The sharp crack from the smaller gun was far worse than the heavier smash of the 4.7s, but each of them caused slight burns, like sunburn.

Below deck, lamp bulbs had smashed and some dishes had jumped out of lockers by the shock of the explosions. Increasing to sixteen knots, she resumed her journey northwards, never staying on the same course for long. At dawn action stations she was still pounding northwards. As the grey dawn lightened the horizon, we saw them. Convoy number two for us, homeward bound from Halifax.

For over four days, in worsening weather, the *Wellington* escorted her convoy home. There were many asdic contacts; there usually were. Each would be carefully investigated, then discarded. Then came one, dead ahead, which gave all the right indications. With a mass of oncoming ships, each heavily laden, there was no alternative. Up went her attack flag, a large, black flag that could not possibly be mistaken for anything else. Her siren, a screeching devil of a thing that would start low and finish on a higher note with each blast, would warn the convoy of what was about to happen. In no time at all they would be alerted and watching. When the Commodore fired his signal rockets, they would turn away from the danger area, leaving it clear for the warship to attack.

On the *Wellington* it was full ahead both engines. She would be at action stations by now and battened down. The first charge from the rails would roll over the stern, released by the levers up on the bridge. The next one would roll off a few seconds later at the same time as the firing bells ordered the throwers off, and even before they hit the water the third one from the rails would complete a diamond shaped pattern of five charges sinking into the sea.

Before the final charge was dropped, the first one would be exploding. The ship would jump like she had been kicked up the backside. Showers of soot would burst out of the funnel and galley chimney. To those sealed below deck, each explosion sounded like a mass of sledge hammers pounding on the ship's side.

Only the people on the bridge and the gun crews would see any of this action, as the depth charge party, usually the anti-aircraft gunners, would be far too busy feeding charges to the dropping point in the rails, or struggling to reload the throwers in time for the next pattern.

From below deck, we would hear crashes as anything that wasn't securely fastened carried away. But the depth charge crews couldn't hold on; they would be far too busy trying to reload in time for the next attack. They wouldn't even see the result of the explosions they were causing.

Sometimes, at full speed and full rudder, she would lean over so far that the low side of her quarterdeck would be forced under water. Foaming sea would boil over everyone and, as it subsided, there would be a quick head count to make sure that no one was missing as the work of reloading was resumed. During such an attack, she would slow, almost stop, listening, and searching. If anyone had the time to look they would see the convoy in the distance almost disappearing over the horizon, but no one would have the time even to wish them well.

These attacks on an echo could last several hours, sometimes all night, but usually ended with losing contact. After searching in a wide circle and finding nothing, it would be full speed ahead after the convoy.

Below decks, we would find light bulbs broken, dishes smashed, tables and forms overturned and sugar and flour liberally sprinkled around once more.

With any luck, we would meet the convoy coming back to find us. With sighs of relief that could almost be heard ashore, they would turn for home again with the *Wellington* in her normal position ahead.

The first aircraft that we saw over the sea put the whole convoy at action stations, but it was not hard to recognise the familiar shape of the Anson as it came towards us. Then it shied away before it came too near as it saw all those guns pointing at it. After allowing enough time for everyone to agree it was friendly, it came on in, and we all waved as it flew low around us. It was only a small speck in the sky as it patrolled, but we felt less lonely as long as we could see it. After it had gone, the sea around seemed a dangerous and inhospitable place. Those who had waved to us from that plane would be home by now, warm, dry and, most of all, safe. Ahead of the *Wellington* was another long night.

Someone asked, "D'you know what day it is?" We had to think about it before becoming aware; all days at sea seemed to be the same.

"Saturday night," he answered his own questions. "What would I be doing on a Saturday night in Civvy Street?" For a while there was a far away look in every eye as silence descended on the gun deck.

Yes, indeed. What would eighteen and nineteen year olds be doing on a Saturday night, when the world was young and free from the shame that was spreading over it.

"When you lot get old," Stripey muttered, bringing us all back to the present, "you'll be proud of this." We stared at him. Sometimes, older people could make such daft remarks.

Then one morning we saw land on each side of us and were surprised to see white snow on the hills. Snowstorms at sea made little difference except to the visibility. When it stopped snowing there would be little trace of it. We had almost forgotten how it could lie on the land.

The *Wellington* was bringing her convoy down through the North Channel between Ireland and Scotland into the Irish Sea. We had our first sight of the Isle of Man in the distance, and we all knew by then that we had seen the last of our home port of Plymouth.

Onwards to the Bar Lightvessel and into the River Mersey: Liverpool. Lovely Liverpool. How glad we were to see you. For most of us, it was our first glimpse of the city. For others, there were wives and families ashore there. We stared wide eyed as the Liver Buildings came into sight. We then backed off towards New Brighton on the other side of the river to let the convoy go on up towards the docks.

The ships passed with waves of farewell; a few blasted away on hooters and whistles, and we waved back. Ashore, on Pier Head, we could see trams, and people were waving to us. Ferries crossed from side to side, and their passengers waved and shouted as they went by. We were all eager to tie up and get off to see Liverpool.

"Hey, Scouse. What are the girls like ashore?"

"Too bloody good for you lot. I wouldn't bother to go ashore if I was you."

"All right. We'll have you instead."

"Gerroff!"

But no such luck. When the convoy had passed, the *Wellington* steamed on towards a large tanker anchored in mid river. The oil tanker was the first stop, and soon we were firmly secured alongside, with fenders between the two ships trying to protect our paintwork from getting too badly marked.

At last she was still. We had almost forgotten what that felt like. There was no need to hold on to things as you walked. No need to balance your plate to keep the food on it. No need to pause warily before moving out onto an open space where there would be nothing to hold on to if she lurched.

The messdecks seemed more crowded than usual, as there was no one on watch now except for a few sentries. The upper deck was the engineers' for the moment, and fuel oil was gushing through pipes into her tanks.

Someone had been expecting us, obviously. There were several sacks of mail waiting. This was always a source of amazement to us. No matter how often orders were changed or how unexpectedly we dropped in somewhere, that was where our mail would be waiting for us.

All around the tables in the mess decks, men sat quietly reading letters from home. It would be the first news we had for weeks. At the end of every voyage this scene would be repeated, one of the most welcome things about coming home.

Just hours later, with full tanks and heavy hearts, the *Wellington* cast off from the tanker and headed seawards with anguished cries from her crew.

"Don't this blasted country have any other escorts besides us?" It looked as if the girls of Liverpool were going to be safe after all. Spirits rose, though, when it became clear we were only going as far as Liverpool Bay to anchor there safely for the night. We thought darkly that the Admiralty must have been aware of our intentions towards the females of the city, and were sending us out there to cool off.

Next morning, and this was it. Look out, Liverpool! There was no hope for you now. Again the *Wellington* slid past the Liver Buildings, but this time, for the benefit of all ashore who cared to look; it was the Royal Navy coming in, with the white ensign fluttering, the crew in smart uniforms, standing motionless in lines on the forecastle and quarterdeck.

Ships at anchor, many of them our convoy of yesterday, remembered their manners and dipped their ensigns in salute, just as a warship was entitled to expect from a merchantman. And our white ensign was dipped in reply as she passed.

Turning in the river, she lined her bows up with the lock, and as the gates opened, she moved in and then waited for the water to equalize. The inner gates opened and we had our first sight of

Gladstone Dock, a big, square dock, with cranes, railway lines and warehouses along all sides of it. This was to be the home of the Navy in Liverpool until the war at sea took us further westwards. One day soon we would see it burning around us, but in the meantime, Britain was buying precious time.

At that period in the history of the Navy, all night shore leave was for men only, and you were not a man until you were twenty-one, or so our Lordships of the Admiralty decreed.

"Your mothers are not here to look after you," they would state joyfully. "They expect us to do that for them. So you lot be back here on board by 11 p.m., or else!"

That was the rules in ships and shore establishments. Be back by 2300. But in Liverpool at that time, it didn't matter. To our dismay, there was no all night shore leave. Only half the ship's company could be allowed ashore at any one time; that was usual and expected. But here, everyone had to be back on board by 1600, and each evening, all the escorts in Gladstone Dock were sent out to anchor near the Bar till next morning. It seemed the Admiralty valued those ships too much to risk having them damaged by air raids.

"What about their crews?" we demanded. "All the girls are working in the afternoons; we can't find any."

There was no doubt the Navy was hard pressed. Convoys with just one lone escort were still being sent to sea and were getting through unscathed. The Atlantic Ocean was a vast area, and a huge convoy would only be the size of a pin head on a ballroom floor to a hunting submarine.

Ships could only operate for so long; then, they would have to stop for boiler cleaning. In the *Wellington's* case, this was every six weeks or so, but she could go on for longer if she had to. These boiler cleaning periods were a desperately needed break for the crews. There would be home leave for some and there was that comforting knowledge that the ship could not suddenly be dispatched to sea with only hours of warning. She would be safely in port for a week or more. We could make dates and reasonably expect to be able to keep them.

Whenever she came into harbour, workmen would swarm over her, repairing, welding, building platforms, adding new bits. Lorry loads of stores would be queuing up to deliver their supplies, and there was always heavy depth charges to roll aboard and find stowage room on the quarterdeck. Cables and pipes would festoon the upper deck and our lovely white decks would soon show the dirt of the land. It was usually a race to get all the work finished by sailing time, and it was not unknown to go to sea with dockyard equipment still aboard. Once, even a startled dockyard workman appeared from somewhere after we had sailed. We put him back on the wall and left him there, shaking his fist after us.

Without much clothes on and unable to reach my locker because a dockyard workman was welding new clips to a nearby deadlight (armour plates that covered the port holes) I tapped him on the shoulder to ask him to get out of the way. He turned, took off his helmet and dark blue glasses and long tresses fell to the collar of her overalls. We grinned appreciatively at each other. The girls of Liverpool sure were all right.

A gunnery school had been established at Ainsdale, just outside the city, and here we practised anti aircraft firing at towed targets. If ever a man was in mortal danger that pilot was. Instructors would tap us on the shoulder when they wanted us to open fire and tap again when it was time to stop. Rapid firing guns would often sever the towing cable, and the drone would float down into the sea accompanied by frantic cheering all round. The aircraft would stream another target, and the instructors would plead, "Don't aim for the wire. Go for the sock".

But there was no satisfaction in that; you couldn't see the hits and as the instructors couldn't see what you were aiming at, it was the towing cable that was mostly the target. If it hadn't broken by the time it had passed along in front of you, you were liable to get carried away and go on shooting, with the target now behind the aircraft as it went into a turn to come back along.

Amid all the welding and riveting, we were still a Naval ship. Liberty men going ashore would fall in on the quarterdeck, or where ever there was room, and be inspected by the Duty Officer before being allowed across the gangway.

All too soon, we could see many ships beginning to gather at anchor out in the river, and later that afternoon, berthing wires were singled up as the *Wellington* made ready for sea. It was Friday the 13th. Dockyard men helped push our gangway aboard.

The *Wellington* backed away from the wall of the dock, and came around gently in a half circle as she lined up for the dock gate. With both ends of the lock open, the way out to the river was now clear, and we felt her stern going down as her screws began to bite. Gathering speed all the time, she steamed along in the centre of the lock heading for the river.

Men on the wall each side of us raised their hands in farewell, and racing along the wall just behind them was Chalky, one of our crew. No matter how swiftly he ran, he couldn't catch up with the *Wellington* as she made for the river.

He was one of those nervous, superstitious characters. He had come from one of the warehouses where, none of us had any doubt, he had been hiding as we cast off from the land. In the Army, he could have been shot for what he had done. Now, knowing we couldn't stop or come back, he was trying to make it look good. We watched without waving as we left him behind, getting smaller and smaller on the dock wall.

What would the charge be that he would have to answer to? Desertion? Cowardice? Absent without leave? And did he think it was worth it to go through the next few weeks without any of his kit and personal belongings? They might have him hanging from a lamp post on the dock entrance when we came back as a warning to all of us in case anybody else had similar ideas.

Our new charges were lining up even before they reached the Bar Lightvessel, but this time there was another escort, a corvette, taking up her position astern.

Once clear of the river the convoy formed into the now familiar lines as we turned northwards making for the North Channel between Ireland and Scotland and heading for the open ocean over the top of Northern Ireland.

Almost as soon as we were clear of the North Channel, the corvette hoisted her attack flag and soon afterwards we could hear the sound of her depth charges banging quite clearly on the *Wellington's* hull, even though she was miles away. This brought home to all of us how devastating these depth charges could be.

We waited anxiously. Was there something waiting for us this time? The North Channel was a well known gateway, so it would be a good place to wait. Should we go back and help the corvette? It was probably the first time for her, while we had some practise at it. But if we went back it would leave the front of the convoy wide open. If there was something ahead of us, they would have a field day.

There was an air of nervousness about the convoy itself; you could feel it. There were no stragglers; everyone was keeping up. As darkness closed over the ships, none were showing any lights. There was no need to cruise down between the lines to warn about open portholes.

The corvette had lost contact astern, and was catching up with the convoy. Before she could regain station, the *Wellington* got a strong echo from out on the port bow, just where it would be if there was something waiting to attack.

This was no time for hesitation. With her siren screaming to warn the *Commodore*, she turned for the target zone, and seconds later the *Commodore* was firing coloured rockets that turned the convoy northwards out of the way.

The echo was strong, and within minutes the attack opened. Travelling at full speed, the first pattern went down and she heeled around, soaking us all as she turned to face the boiling sea erupting behind her.

Target moving left: depth setting 500 feet. We could hear the full ahead gongs down in the engine room and feel her stern going down as she forged ahead. Barely giving her time to reach full speed, the firing bells were sending the next pattern away, leaving her dangerously close to the erupting explosions.

All through the night the *Wellington* attacked that echo, until just after dawn we lost all trace of it. After searching for several hours it was full ahead once more after a long vanished convoy. It was dinner time before we saw wisps of smoke beyond the horizon and another hour before we saw the corvette in our usual position at the head of the mass of shipping.

If those depth charge attacks on the echoes that occurred from time to time served no other purpose, they certainly trained the crews of the convoy escorts. No one can be sure they did not ward off intended offences, or caused damage that prevented future attacks. Something was learnt from each of them, building skill and experience into a fighting ship.

HMS *Wellington* was a warship now, with a warship's crew. As the time of Dunkirk drew near, she would soon have to prove it.

Chapter Three

No one was sure what was to happen next as the *Wellington* came to anchor close to the white cliffs of Dover. So far, we hadn't lost any ships while in convoy, but while coming home with a mass of ships from Halifax we had run into floating mines in the North Channel, the first we had ever seen.

After warning the convoy, it had been quite exciting destroying the mines. Lewis machine guns mounted on the bridge and on each side of the wheelhouse sank a few, while many of us lay on the upper deck with our rifles cuddled into our shoulders, barrels resting on the lower guard rails and boxes of .303 ammunition from the magazines below beside us. When enough holes had been shot in them, they would sink. Sometimes, if you aimed very carefully, you would hit one of the horns; then it would explode almost as violently as one of our depth charges. But this explosion would be on the surface, and bits of metal would go whistling everywhere. To us youngsters it was all very satisfying. When we couldn't find any more, the convoy would steam on again.

While in the Irish Sea and still a long way from home, we had been ordered to abandon the convoy and proceed at full speed to Dover. Ships of all sizes were beginning to gather around us as the *Wellington* moved uneasily in the Channel swell. Just before dark, the anchor was heaved in and, free of the land, she turned toward the French coast, where the distant sound of rumbling guns and a constant flicker like lightening just over the horizon seemed to be warning everyone to stay away.

With hearts beating faster we blew up our lifebelts under our coats and adjusted our steel helmets. This was the first time they had been out of their lockers, and the straps needed altering before they would fit comfortably. Knowing that no one would sleep tonight, we admired each other mirthlessly, wishing our girls could see us now.

Dawn found us off Le Havre, as we closed the land we could see people on the rocks waving and calling. Small motor boats that seemed to be waiting nearby began moving in to take them off as soon as they saw that we were watching. Beyond the rocks was a green field, and from some trees in the far corner of it we saw streams of red dots spitting out, and splashes began appearing among the boats moving towards the people on the rocks.

Not until we heard the sound of the explosions did we realise it was shellfire we were seeing, but within seconds the *Wellington's* 4.7s began answering back and we were quite near enough to see the flame and smoke as our shells landed.

Instantly, several streams of red dots curved out of that field, aimed now at the *Wellington*. There was no other ship in sight; it had to be us. But at least the small boats were being left free to do their work.

We could hear the shells passing close by, making a noise like a headmaster's cane as it came down on your hand. Some of them were bursting so close that water was splashing our decks. Bits of metal seemed to be pinging on our sides. A hole appeared low down in the wall of the Captain's pantry, shrapnel penetrated inside and cut a jagged hole in a bucket of dirty water the Captain's steward had left there. A wire stay to the funnel was cut through by shrapnel and the wire swung loose dangerously until someone secured it. Several holes appeared in the funnel that allowed smoke to come out.

One of the crew of A gun was knocked off his feet by a piece of metal that thudded into the cork lifebelt he was wearing in addition to his Mae West. The metal was almost red hot, and smoking. The tip of it had reached his skin, and he was thrashing about as if he was mortally wounded. When the First Aid party reached him and held him down as they tore off the lifebelt, all they saw was a pin head burn.

But things were not all that pleasant ashore either. The top end of the field seemed to be all on fire as the *Wellington's* guns sent salvoe after salvoe into it. The magazines were supplying two kinds of shells, armour piercing, which we were using now, and now and again, a time fused shell would be sent off as a present to anyone stupid enough to be out in the open, and we would see the red, burning black bursts among the trees.

The red dots had stopped coming, and the small boats went about their business of taking everybody off that was in sight. The *Wellington* waited until all the boats were well out of gunfire range, then she moved on.

Further along the coast at St Valery we saw an opening in a cliff that led in to a harbour. Small boats were pouring out loaded with people, and unloading them onto other ships waiting outside. *The Wellington* nosed in, and we steamed up a channel that widened into a basin in front of a village. Fishing boats, decked in flags as if it was a regatta day, were loading people carrying bundles of belongings. Just behind them were many large, round oil tanks, sitting there, as if waiting to be destroyed. What a target for our ready guns they would have made and what a catastrophe it would have been for all those people if the *Wellington* had accepted it.

We turned there, just clear of the boats, and made our way out again. Just as we reached the sea something opened fire on us from the headland on our right. Almost at the same moment, we saw the flashes of gunfire coming from the cliff top on the left.

Turning right at full speed to engage the battery on our starboard side, we saw a destroyer nosing in from seaward taking on the battery on the left. For nearly fifteen minutes both ships smashed broadsides into the cliff tops at the entrance of St Valery as those fishing boats, still with all their flags flying, poured those people out to the waiting ships.

I wonder how many of those people waiting for evacuation from St Valery remembers seeing HMS *Wellington* coming in to look at them. And did they hold their breath and pray as she looked at those oil tanks and left them so that they could live? And how many of them got safely away because of the gun batteries at the harbour entrance that she engaged and destroyed?

We saw many German aircraft during this time, but mostly they were high up and showed no particular interest in us. The *Wellington* only opened fire at one when a tug nearby was attacked. The awful crack from the 3 inch anti aircraft gun was much worse than the heavier 4.7s.

The next night at Fecamp, every boat the *Wellington* had was lowered into the water. With the motor boats towing the seaboats and the carley floats secured behind, they moved off into the darkness along with seventeen of our crew with instructions to load as many survivors as possible and get them out to any ship they could find.

Not long after they had gone, searchlights were suddenly switched on ashore and began lighting up the boats. But not for long. It took two broadsides from the 4.7s to put them out. The first one missed by inches; we saw the dust fly up in front of the lights. They went out immediately the second salvoe landed.

We cruised that coast all night with increasing anxiety without once seeing our boats. Gunfire would erupt without warning at different places along the darkened coast, and we wondered and worried about who was being shot at. We stayed close in, inviting retaliation, but none came.

Next afternoon near Dieppe, we met a cruiser nosing slowly shorewards. Feeling much safer with her behind us, we went in with her, but she needed more water than we did and she was soon just a shadow in the mist behind.

The land looked like a solid cliff, with fields sloping upwards to a road beyond. We were near enough now to see that the road was full of vehicles all moving from left to right.

Were they our boys retreating? Or someone else advancing?

They were too far away for any of us to be sure what they were, and it was not easy to stand and wait as the *Wellington* pressed on towards the land. Then, quite clearly, small objects that through our binoculars we identified as tanks turned off the road and trundled down through the field. Those red dots that we knew all about by now began curving outwards.

There was no doubt who they were now, and they were good shots too. We could feel and hear the same things happening all over again.

The *Wellington* turned aside so that all guns could bear, and broadside after broadside was dispatched shorewards at the tanks. Even the gun barrels began to burn as our lovely paintwork caught fire. Over and above the sound of our gunfire and the exploding shells all around us there came a new sound, like express trains passing close overhead, as our big brother just behind us lashed out at what was up in those fields. I believe that cruiser was HMS *Cardiff.* In no time at all there was nothing to be seen of the field except fire and smoke.

We had quickly learnt how to tell the difference between our own aircraft and the German; our fighters had black and white stripes on their wings, which was a brilliant idea, as you could spot them instantly high in the sky. The noise of aircraft was there all the time.

After four days, with no boats or ammunition left, low on fuel and seeing nothing moving, we turned away for home. For four nights and four days corned beef sandwiches and jugs of tea had been organised by the Repair and First Aid parties below decks and thrust up through a hastily opened watertight hatch when things seemed quiet. For four days our lifebelts had been kept blown up and our steel helmets firmly on.

On the journey back across the Channel, the gun crews slept on the deck around their guns, while the throb of aircraft engines filled the sky. One passing too near brought everyone to their feet. The open fire bells were only seconds away as the sound began to fade.

We were nearly home, but it was not a happy return. We had lost seventeen of our crew. No one had seen or heard anything of them since they had moved away in the dark off Fecamp.

The ship came alive to the piped order, "Hands to stations for entering harbour." We came into Portsmouth steaming past silent crowds watching from the wall, seeing the fire-blackened guns and empty boat davids as she swept past. As she manoeuvred towards her berth her siren suddenly shrieked. As we looked to see what she was shouting about, we saw a small tug coming towards us from across the dock with our missing crew waving and shouting.

The lines of sailors on her forecastle and quarterdeck wavered as they saw their shipmates; they started to wave back, then stiffened as they remembered. This was Portsmouth, a Naval port. Shoulders squared and heads came up as they held their ranks. They were whole again; battle-scarred but intact. If the Admiral had been watching from the signal tower, he would have seen a small warship coming in with smoke-blackened guns, no boats left and an unshaven looking crew. But her white ensign was flying and she proudly saluted the tower with her crew standing silently in line, then berthed on the wall as expertly as the Admiral could have wished.

Below deck there was absolute chaos. This was the first time the watertight doors had been opened since we had left Dover. Almost every light bulb in the ship was smashed. Tables and forms were cracked. Broken dishes poured like water out of lockers as soon as the doors were opened. Flour and sugar smothered the messes.

We looked with dismay at the shambles we had made of our home. A small tanker was shouting for somebody to take her wires as she tried to come alongside with fuel for us. Lorries were beginning to arrive with ammunition and stores. From across the dock a small motor launch was making towards us, towing a long line of replacement boats and rafts.

If our seventeen so called survivors thought they were entitled to a hero's welcome, they were rudely awakened, claiming they had taken people off all through the night and had been taken aboard just after daylight by a tug after an unfriendly aircraft kept coming to look at them. The tug had arrived here yesterday.

"We haven't slept for three nights," they complained. "We thought you lot had been sunk." They seemed to be disappointed to see us here, safe and afloat, probably thinking about survivors leave.

"You poor sods! Our hearts bleed for you. Three nights without sleep? There, there, then. We'll make it all up to you tonight. You can all turn in an hour earlier."

Good natured banter, but deeper inside we all knew we were a much more dangerous ship now. HMS *Wellington* was a fighting ship and well able to respond. There was a pride of possession, and of belonging. She was ours to aim and to guide. The steel helmets around the guns had our initials painted in them. The catches on the the ready use ammunition lockers had been sandpapered and greased. It would not take minutes to be able to open fire after the alarm bells had sounded in future; seconds would be enough.

We no longer walked down ladders; we slid down with hands on the polished brass handrails and feet clear of the step. Anyone coming up learnt to leap aside whenever a boot approached from above.

It was the same below decks. Watertight doors and hatches would be slammed shut as soon as the last backside had raced through. There was an air of confidence that had not been there before. Her crew knew that they and their ship was as good as any. It didn't matter that someone had put grease on the ladder handrails and you came down much faster than you had intended. You were part of a family. You belonged, and proudly so.

To our lasting regret, we didn't get to see Portsmouth. All of the available escorts had been withdrawn from the North Atlantic to assist with the evacuation from France, and now they were being sent back to convoy work as soon as they were refuelled. That same day, as if they guessed our intentions, the Admiralty ordered the *Wellington* out of Portsmouth while their girls were still safe and we nosed back out of the harbour and headed down Channel towards Plymouth and Land's End, without even a chance of dating any of the girls of Dover or Portsmouth. Our fire blackened guns, which we had regarded as medals to our exploits, were repainted without anyone, except the onlookers at Portsmouth, having a chance to see them and marvel at our courage.

"Invisible paint," grinned Mick, as he painted one of the barrels. "I've put sand in it. It'll all fall off before we reach Liverpool." It didn't, and when our Petty Officer noticed the gritty gun barrel he made Mick scrape it all off and do it again, properly this time.

It felt just like coming home again as we steamed up the Mersey. This time, to our delight, we were not chased out at dusk to anchor in safety at the Bar. Now we could stay and take our chance like the rest of the people of Liverpool.

Sitting on a bollard on the dockside was Chalky. He had no kit with him. How could he? It was still here on the *Wellington*. He told us later that the base had accepted his explanation of how he had missed his ship. He had been issued with a steaming bag and some spare kit, put aboard a trawler and sent to sea the same night we sailed.

We grinned. Much better than hanging him, we thought.

Shore leave at last in Liverpool. We licked our lips. But the grins were soon wiped away. "There are some bad women in Liverpool", grinned our Jaunty, the ship's policeman. "They've been waiting to eat you lot. Can't 'ave that. Your mothers will write and complain to the Admiral. I shall be waiting for you 'ere at this gangway, at eleven o'clock. That's late enough for anyone to be out."

To get back aboard a ship in Gladstone Dock from somewhere in the city by eleven o'clock used to take some doing. Like Cinderella, we would suddenly become aware of the time and stare at each other in horror. Then to the consternation of whoever it was we were with we would start to run off in fright. Visions of the Jaunty standing hopefully at the ships gangway with an axe in one hand and a watch in the other would spur us on. No tram or the elevated railway could do that journey faster than we would. We soon learnt the quickest way to take and, to our credit, were never late, or adrift as it was called.

Only half the ships company was ashore at any one time. To make it up to us for all the weeks spent at sea, shore leave was usually from twelve noon until 0800 next morning. Not for the under twenty ones though; for them, it was always 2300.

Though not knowing for sure when sailing time would be, we would have a pretty good idea. Four days was the usual time in harbour between convoys, unless the ship was due a boiler clean; then she could be in port for up to ten days. Half the ship's company could then be sent home on leave; the other half would have their turn next time.

We found it easy to find girl friends ashore but hard to keep them. We could leave port in a hurry and no one knew for sure when we would be back. Many lovely friendships were broken by a ship sailing early, as we had no means of telling our girls not to turn up.

With France defeated it didn't take Germany long to move their Naval bases to the Atlantic seaboard. The Atlantic was the next battleground where they intended to meet us head on. It would not be safe to disperse our convoys in mid ocean for much longer. German submarines would be able to range outwards with us no matter how far we took them.

One afternoon in mid ocean, we watched as over fifty ships broke away from us and went on their different courses. Feeling like mother without her children we cruised northwards on a zig-zag course at any easy speed, with time to waste, until we collected the homegoing convoy from Canada two days later.

In the darkness of early morning, well before dawn, there were two flashes over the Western horizon reported by all lookouts. The convoy we had escorted out here had long gone on their separate ways. These flashes could not have come from one of them. The new convoy was too far to the northwards to be responsible for this.

It could have been lightening, but somehow it didn't look like that.

Turning away from her northerly course, the *Wellington* increased speed to full ahead to investigate the cause of the flashes we had seen.

There was not so much grumbling this time at dawn action stations, as everyone could feel and hear the speed she was making. Men did more than go through the motions. Ready use lockers were opened and guns were loaded.

Full daylight and nothing in sight as the *Wellington* bumped onwards through an increasingly choppy sea. Then, far ahead, the lookout reported a number of small black dots that soon resolved into ship's lifeboats as we raced towards them. They were not small lifeboats either, we noted, as we neared them. They were bigger than anything we carried. Lifeboats of a liner, six of them, full of people waving madly to us. Men, women and children were there.

We waved back in astonishment as we swept by well clear of them, without reducing speed, and circled, watching, listening. If that submarine was sitting under those boats, we were going to be an easy target for it when we stopped to pick them up.

In the scuppers along each side of the low quarterdeck we had scrambling nets rolled up ready for situations like this. These were cut loose and dropped over so they hung down to the water on each side.

We hardly needed telling to be quick and stay alert. Still moving quite fast the ship headed for the last boat in the line. Through the loud hailer on the bridge, we told them to keep going as fast as they could. Crew members got down on the nets and waited ready as we came up on the first one. A tow rope was ready and made fast in seconds by our own crew who were now in the boat.

Those who were able to scrambled up the net as we towed the boat along with us. Women were helped up, children lifted up. Within minutes the boat was empty and being cast off, but not before we had snatched boxes of corned beef and tinned milk, which were the lifeboats' emergency rations.

We nearly left Fred behind as he went after the last box of milk. He missed the box and had to leap for the net as we forged ahead towards the next boat. If he had missed that net he would have been mince meat in the screws.

The next boat was drawing alongside, and again it was the same routine. Each of those boats had been well equipped with emergency rations. A big pile of boxes were stacking on our quarterdeck, but they were going to be desperately needed to feed all these people. The last boat was now alongside. Over a hundred and fifty souls had been taken aboard.

We all knew that the submarine that had done this was probably watching from a safe distance. If he could get the angle right, he might well chance a couple of his torpedoes. At our snails speed he had a sitting target. Many anxious eyes were searching the sea around us. The last of the survivors was being lifted aboard as the sound of the engine room telegraphs calling for full speed ahead was a signal to hold our breath. It would be now or never. Down went her stern, and a white churning wave built up behind her as her screws thrust the water away with a roar.

With nothing else to vent our feelings on, we opened fire on the lifeboats and reduced them to matchwood within seconds. Perhaps the noise of the gunfire would produce something, we half hoped he would chance a shot at us to give his position away.

With the scrambling nets lashed back in the scuppers we turned for home, with HMS *Wellington* laden much more than usual.

We had on board all that was left of the *Highland Patriot*, a Royal Mail steamship of over 14000 tons bound independently from South America to the U.K. The journey back to safety was a nightmare to everyone except the children. There was not one nook or cranny, passage or corner, that was not occupied by someone. To move about at night, when all the lower decks were covered with sleeping bodies, was well nigh impossible. Gun crews took to spending all night trying to sleep in the turrets; they could hardly get any nearer their place of duty than that.

One man struggled to reach the heads to relieve himself, only to find after a nightmare journey across the bodies, four men asleep sitting on the pans, their heads pillowed on the straining bars.

Chef and his helpers worked all night, but after just one day there was no flour left. Bread was something we had better keep for the children.

Up on deck we had the potato locker which was a large metal affair with doors at the top to empty the sacks in and a small sliding door at the bottom to shovel the spuds out. When this was full, it could hold all of two tons of potatoes, enough to last us three weeks in normal times. After two days, only protesting sailors were being shovelled out.

From deep in the stores some sacks of rice were hauled out.

Our staple diet soon became boiled rice and corned beef.

As passengers on the *Highland Patriot*, these people had been used to having their meals served to them and given a choice of menus. But here, such was the crush that there had to be three sittings on each of our small tables for every meal. When the first sitting had finished eating they got up and left. The next sitting came and looked at the dirty dishes and waited for us to do something about it. With tongues in cheek, the off duty crew rolled their sleeves up, washed the dishes, opened more tins of corned beef, collected more hot, boiled rice from the galley, made more steaming tea, then stood politely by while the second sitting cleared their plates.

It was then our survivors called a halt and held a meeting. From then on we were the ones who were waited on. We would uneasily find our corned beef and rice waiting for us when we came off watch; our dirty dishes would be washed for us. Soon we felt like the passengers and our survivors seemed more like the crew.

The children had the time of their lives. They were dressed in our uniforms, they steered the ship, tried to fire our guns, drop our depth charges, and often unexpectedly joined a startled lookout in the crow's nest.

After three days of steady steaming we rounded the Mull of Kintyre and headed up into the Firth of Clyde. When Gourock came in sight there was no way we could stand in line on the forecastle and quarterdeck as a warship coming into harbour should have done. As we closed the wall, onlookers must have thought we were some kind of secret weapon to be carrying such a huge crew.

We had all dug into our lockers to provide clothes for the passengers. There was such a large number of people on the upper deck that we were lost in the crowd. We had to plead with them not to all stand on one side as the *Wellington* listed alarmingly when we berthed her alongside the wall.

There were buses and a long line of ambulances waiting for us as a camera with a Pathe News badge on it filmed it all. There were handshakes and hugs as they filed ashore. Men with stretchers came aboard to collect the injured. Two little girls were discovered just in time hiding in A gun turret; they wanted to come back to sea with us. Kisses were thrown as the buses moved away.

Whether that film was ever shown in cinemas we would never know. Our eyes glazed as we thought of our girls sitting in the cinema back home, sitting on their own of course, or with another girl friend, and suddenly jumping out of their seat with astonishment at seeing us on the screen right there in front of them.

"Let's shoot up the ambulance," Fred whispered, "It'll look great in the Gaumont". As I stared at him he said, "There's nobody in it, even the driver is waving to the buses."

But Pathe had stopped filming. They had to make way for the lorries, the inevitable lorries carrying potatoes, flour, rice, corned beef, tinned milk. It was all there, and the mail. Whoever was responsible for that mail could not have had much warning this time. Yet here it was, waiting for us to arrive, just as usual.

On the river side a small tanker was coming to tie up on the *Wellington*. She had to be fed as well. Give us two hours and if we had to, we could be ready for sea again.

From that time on, round about every Christmas, a large whicker basket would be delivered to the dockside at HMS *Wellington*, no matter where she was. It was a Christmas hamper inscribed 'From the grateful survivors of the *Highland Patriot*'.

"Shore leave for the Port Watch from 1700," came the pipe. So we were not going straight back out to get that convoy from Canada.

"Feel like a pint, Fred?"

"I'd rather go to sleep," he said, voicing the desire of most of us. "But we can do that tonight. Gourock or Glasgow?"

I grinned, sleep forgotten. "Ask Scotty there, he's from these parts.

"What are the girls like in Scotland, Scotty?"

"Too bloody good for you lot. I wouldn't bother to g . . . ."

"We know, we know," we would interrupt, well used to the local's fierce determination to protect their females from us. "Good job your father didn't feel the same way you do. How far from Glasgow are we?"

"About an hour."

"We'll have two of your lasses on our arm before you can get your kilt on, and we hope they're your sisters."

CHAPTER FOUR

Glasgow lived up to all that we had heard about it. There we saw the finest acts on the stage of the Empire Theatre and marvelled at the price reached for an onion, in short supply in those days.

We soon found ourselves girls. They were very understanding when we would suddenly clap our hands to our mouths in fright as the clocks striking warned us that the witching hour was nigh. We had their addresses, we could write.

"See you the day after tomorrow, under the clock", we would call as we raced away. "Wait for us".

What a difficult place Gourock was to get back to from Glasgow by 2300. And how bitter we felt two days later as we prepared for sea. As the bow of the *Wellington* bit into the cold water of the North Channel and we sheltered in the lee of the after gun turret, we thought of our girls waiting under the clock for their fellers that wouldn't be turning up.

"Never trust a sailor," they would be saying angrily, and who could blame them. But perhaps they would understand. It meant nothing to us that a convoy homeward bound from Canada was under attack, or that we would have been there with them had it not been for the *Highland Patriot*.

We shook the rain off our oilskins and tried to keep our binoculars dry under our coats. Back there in Glasgow there would be trams full of people; dances, films, laughter, fun. Here where we were it was cold and wet, as dark as we could make it, and there was a warning in every flash of white foam. There would be sleepless nights and fear that would twist your stomach.

"Know what day it is?" asked Fred quietly.

I nodded in the darkness, though no one could see. "I know, Saturday". For a long while the rain on our faces went unheeded. Then the telephone on the bulkhead down on the quarterdeck began to wail and the Leading Seaman of the Watch went down the ladder from the shelter of the turret to answer it.

"There's a submarine coming up behind us, it's one of ours," he warned. "She'll stay close till we're well out. Report when you've got her."

We leaned back against the gun turret to steady ourselves as we searched for her through our dry binoculars. She took some finding, as all there was to see was a wet black conning tower on a wet black night.

I saw her first. Now that I knew where to look and what she looked like it was easy to see her. But nobody else could. A disbelieving Leading Seaman reported by telephone to the bridge that a submarine no one could see was coming up astern.

A blasphemous voice asked, "If you can't bloody well see it, how the !!***!!* hell d'you know it's there?"

Just about then, a dim blue light winked from the darkness, and now everyone could see it. She fell into line astern, close enough to throw a spud at. No one needed binoculars to see her in the darkness close to our stern now.

Some thirty minutes later, one of the crew from the wheelhouse was sent aft to read the log, quite a normal event. But he had come from the wheelhouse; no one had bothered to tell them about a submarine that was nibbling at our stern like a trout being reeled in by a fisherman.

Leaning on the gun turret for shelter from the wind and rain and to steady ourselves as the *Wellington* pitched and shuddered, we watched him read the log and write down the numbers on a signal pad he was carrying. Then he dropped it as he caught sight of the submarine. It never crossed our minds that he was unaware of our sub. As he jumped up and down and screamed "Submarine!" we thought there was another one.

"Where!"

"There! You're all bloody blind!"

Frantic searching through our binoculars. "What bearing?"

"There. Look. She's ramming us!"

When it was eventually sorted out, he would forever after be known as Subby.

After two days of steaming at high speed into a head wind, regardless of damage being caused, we reached the homeward bound convoy from Halifax that had been under attack for the last forty eight hours. Just two corvettes had been attacking an increasing number of contacts for the last four days, and you could almost feel the relief as they handed over command to HMS *Wellington* as she took up her station ahead of the mass of ships.

Several times the Admiralty changed the route of the convoy. We all knew what that meant. They must have gathered information that danger was forming ahead of this convoy and they were trying to guide us around it.

A Sunderland flying boat stayed with us long after she should have departed, but finally we were on our own; just two corvettes and us, and a slow and lumbering convoy of heavily laden merchantmen steamed resolutely on into the dangerous darkness.

As night formed its screen around the horizon it felt like the lowering of the house lights in a theatre in readiness for the show to begin, except that no one was looking forward to the beginning of this show.

Supper that night was a silent affair and it was soon over, as nobody seemed to be hungry. Lifebelts were more in evidence than usual. Not blown up, but no one seemed to have forgotten to wear his this time, as usually happened. Without having to be reminded, upper deck crews checked their weather clothes ready for the night watches, as once those watertight doors were slammed shut there would be no coming back for a coat someone had left behind.

It was still early evening, but pitch dark, when the asdics picked up the sound of a torpedo running. There was just enough time to blast out a warning on the siren and we heard the corvette astern doing the same, before the thing struck. It hit the third ship in the centre column.

Every vessel in the convoy would have seen the flash of the explosion and the stricken ship turned sideways out of line, while the rest of the convoy gritted its teeth and lumbered on past her. Almost at once came flash number two from further back in the line.

Jesus! He must be in amongst the convoy.

It was pointless trying to hide in the darkness now; they had found us. The 4.7s began blasting time fused star shells, hoping that someone would see him on the surface and try to ram. Each of the escorts were steaming at full speed between the lines of ships; if he was at periscope depth it would be highly dangerous for him to remain there; he would have to go down. There were boats in the water with survivors from the two ships that had been hit. There was wreckage and floating cargo. How many men had died on those ships? Most of the engine and boiler room crews, we had no doubt.

Within minutes, it was all being left astern, like some monstrous board game being cleared ready to restart the next round.

Several times during that night heavy attacks on asdic contacts were carried out, all of them ending with lost contact.

One of the corvettes had picked up the survivors from the two ships that had been hit and sunk during the night. Soon after dawn the welcome Sunderland came back on station. They could hardly have had many hours of rest during that night. But then, they were no worse off than we were.

The tension of the night began to ease and it was at that moment the torpedo struck. It hit a big ship in the outside line. She reeled sideways, belching smoke and flame and our asdic made contact close in on the starboard quarter. As the *Wellington* lunged to attack, the convoy rapidly altered course away from the contact area, and we spared a fleeting moment to cheer as we saw that torpedoed ship turning back into line and trying to catch up.

Later that afternoon the *Wellington* steamed up through the lines of ships to come up on the injured member. There was a huge hole in her side from just below deck level to below the water line, big enough to drive a double decker bus through. Hundreds of black barrels were stacked up inside, with water washing all around them now. Every so often some would swirl around and float out. We looked soundlessly at a line of black barrels dotted away into the distance behind us like a line of cat's eyes marking a road.

Should we take off her crew and sink her, so ending the paper chase? But we were looking at only one hold; she had several others, each just as full. Britain desperately needed whatever it was she was carrying, or she wouldn't be carrying it.

What the hell! They knew where we were. There was no longer any point in trying to cover our tracks. Let her sail on.

Through our loud hailer on the bridge we asked, "Do you need any help?"

"I've lost a lot of fuel; we're burning furniture. Sorry about the smoke."

Regaining station ahead it was almost a relief to make a strong asdic contact right in the path of the convoy, just where it could be expected if there was something laying in wait for that mass of shipping to pass over it. The black attack flag went up with a thump that nearly shook the mast. Like well drilled guardsmen our convoy turned smartly away out of the danger zone, while the *Wellington* sprinkled depth charges around like a maddened gardener scattering seeds.

It was well into the night and the convoy was far out of sight before we gave up and took off after them, following their trail of barrels as easily as if following a herd of elephants.

Whether it did any harm to the submarines that had gathered around us we will never know, but it did a power of good to the crew of HMS *Wellington* to be able to vent their anger on something, be it only an echo.

Desperately short of depth charges, we restocked from one of the ships in the convoy. With fangs bared once more, resumed our place at the head of the line.

No further attacks developed, but for this time the Mersey turned out to be as dangerous as the open ocean. Mines had been laid in the approaches to Liverpool and, though the minesweepers had done their part before we arrived, these were mines that no one had come across before. You didn't have to hit them; just to pass near them was enough.

Howls of laughter went up when we first saw our crew members from Southern Ireland leaving the ship to go on home leave. They were the only members of the crew allowed to wear civvies. As Ireland was officially neutral, they could not wear uniform when going home. How strange and different they looked. They shook their fists and threatened dire revenge when they returned as our insults followed them until they were out of sight along the quay. Ireland might have been neutral, but many of her young men fought by our sides. I never knew of any that did not return from leave, often with more in those suitcases than when they went.

The ship seemed oddly quiet, and much bigger after they had gone. There was room to stretch at the messdeck tables for dinner. If someone shouted you could hear it all along the ship. There seemed to be plenty of sugar and many tins of Ideal milk.

When the Bosun's Mate came round piping shore leave from 1300, it was a relief.

"Let's go," said Fred. And I needed no urging.

Across the dock, a large freighter was being unloaded. Crates of oranges were being slung across from the ship to the shore by the dockside cranes. Large, luscious oranges were rolling around from smashed crates as we walked by.

A man thrust an armful of these fruits on to each of us. As we couldn't walk out through the dockyard gates carrying that lot we had to turn back to our ship with them.

A grinning Jaunty holding a charge sheet was waiting at the gangway for us. "Stealing fruit," he chortled, "I've oiled the key of the cells for you two." Then as we protested, "I know, I know, I saw it. Take them below then get off with you." So he was human after all.

"Here, you have them." We dumped them on the deck in front of him and beat a hasty retreat. Fred couldn't resist speaking loudly to an imaginary policeman behind a nearby railway truck.

"Constable, that man up there has been pinching oranges," pointing to the startled Jaunty. Then we raced off before anything else could befall us.

"We should have asked him for all night leave," I gasped, when we were safely out of sight. "He was in the mood to grant it."

"Never mind," grinned Fred, fingering the down on his chin. "We'll soon be men."

I grinned back at him. We were nineteen. Wouldn't be long now. What wild nights of passionate love was conjured up when at last we would be entitled to all night leave, when the Navy would no longer be able to protect us for our mothers.

We set our caps at an angle and tugged our lanyards into place. Although we were not really used to walking into public houses yet, much preferring to go to the pictures, we walked straight into the first pub we came to in Lime Street.

Too late to back out with dignity, we grinned sickly at the two ladies who were holding out their arms for us. Even as I hesitated, Fred was already disappearing into an ample bosom as she hauled him close. The other one held out her glass to me with, "Gin and tonic, dear, a double if you don't mind." I took her glass round the corner, went straight into the toilet and climbed out through the window. About seven minutes later, Fred came out through the same window and we hared off towards the safety of Lime Street station.

With a meal of egg and chips – it was always egg and chips, or egg, chips and sausage if you were lucky – under our belts, we felt brave enough to slink into a pub, after a quick look round the door, for two half pints of beer, in pint glasses, we demanded, as it looked more manly. Then it was to the cinema to see a film. As we came out, we realised our witching hour was near if we wanted to be home in time to avoid trouble. Just as we set off the air raid sirens started.

"We could take shelter," mused Fred. "They can hardly charge us with being adrift if there's an air raid."

"We'd have to spend the whole night in an air raid shelter. Or did you make other plans in that pub?" I demanded suspiciously.

"Hell!" protested Fred. "She was older than my grannie."

Not fancying sitting all night on a bench in a shelter, we decided to return to the *Wellington*. Every time we passed the entrance to a shelter there were figures outside who asked us where we were going, and each time we would reply, "Back to our ship." And they would let us go on.

The city was quiet as it waited, as if girding its loins for what was to come. There was a moon and some clouds; it wasn't truly dark but the roads were empty and deserted as we hurried along.

Then we could hear them, that low, pulsating drone that seemed to vibrate into doorways and shake glass windows in the nearby buildings. As we began to run we could hear the bombs coming down. There were the flashes that lit up the roofs of the city, and the earth shaking crunch as they hit.

The flashes suddenly became much more frequent as the anti aircraft defences came into action, like a constant ripple of lightning that seemed to be coming from everywhere. We could hear things dropping on the roofs and roads around us like somebody throwing handfuls of ball bearings. Holding our gas mask haversacks on our heads as protection from this shrapnel we ran on, stopping to crouch against a wall or press into a doorway as a screech came too near. Fires seemed to be raging all over the city, and once we stopped to look back at what seemed to be a church sending up a huge pillar of flame and sparks.

There were large, red glows coming from the docks; those aircraft would have little difficulty in finding them in this moonlight with the river to guide them. We stopped for a moment in dismay as we rounded the corner of a warehouse. A huge fire was lighting up the warships like a Guy on Bonfire Night.

We ran up the gangway sweating and breathless. It must have been the first time we had ever been thirty minutes early and promptly fell over the hoses that had been run out over the upper deck to deal with any fires that might start. The city seemed to be all on fire. After a while it became possible to distinguish between gun flashes and bomb flashes. Through our binoculars, it was also possible to see the fire fighters still working through all this; we could see their jets of water around every fire.

Temporarily blinded by a nearby flash and explosion we made our way down to the mess deck. Hammocks had been slung and we did the same, but I didn't feel much like sleeping. Feeling afraid but ashamed to show it, I joined the other brave souls in the warm and well lit galley; a kettle of cae was simmering on the range. Conversation would stop for a moment as the place would rattle from a near hit, then would go hurrying on again as we tried to console each other from the senseless destruction that was going on outside.

Whenever there seemed to be a lull, some of us would go up topsides and stare at the fires that seemed to envelop the city. As if there was a limit to the fear that one could feel, the numbers in the galley began to dwindle as men turned in. From the safety of my hammock I listened to a heavy anti aircraft battery that seemed to be firing from somewhere nearby on the river. Occasionally we would hear the screech of a falling bomb, and I would clutch the bar above my head and feel the ship tremble quietly, as the earth from which this dock was made shook under the explosions.

From further along the mess deck I saw Fred's hands on the bar above his head. I could hear our, by now well-known, ball bearings dropping on the deck just above my head. Sentries from the duty watch were posted up there, so if a fire did start, we would be quickly turfed out.

I awoke with reluctance, surprised that it was morning and everything was as normal as usual. There were no gaping holes or bodies laying about, but there was a strong smell of burning wood as smoke from the city drifted past.

From the upper deck, men could be seen arriving for work just as if nothing had happened. Pretending to be just as unconcerned, we reeled up our hoses and put them away.

In the mail that morning came a letter from Lorna in Plymouth. I had met her while in Training Division. She was tall, dark, with twinkling eyes that could wink at a passing stranger while she was arm in arm with me. Her figure in a bathing suit gave a young sailor ideas that could keep him awake at night. I had met her while I was swimming for the raft moored just off the bathing pool at Plymouth Hoe. I thought she was drowning and went to her aid, with perhaps undue alacrity, I suppose. As she said later, "How would you react if a strange man tried to tear off your bathing suit?"

She hadn't been drowning, just floating. "I wouldn't have kicked him in the b . . . er, where you kicked me," I protested. It had ended with her having to tow me to the raft.

I hadn't been able to tell her that we were leaving Plymouth.

Like always, she had to be left to turn up for a date that I could not keep. And when at last I was able to write, I couldn't tell her where we were. Our letters had to be posted on the ship and were censored there too.

And now here was Lorna, telling me the family she was working for had moved to a place called Southport. "No use you looking for me around Plymouth," she scolded, "I'll be swimming at Southport Hoe. And I won't be swimming alone, so there!"

The thought of that lovely body swimming close to anyone except me sent waves of emotion coursing through my overalls. Southport? That was up this way somewhere.

"Hey, Scouse. Where's Southport?"

"Southport? About an hour or so on the electric train. You're dribbling."

I wiped my chin. "No I'm not. I was just anticipating." Next time ashore I knew where Fred and I would be going. Perhaps we could get away from the bombing by going outside of Liverpool, but we would still have to be back on board by 2300. Blast it! Why couldn't we be men sooner? It would be much safer. Our mothers would not be pleased with the Navy if they made us run home through an air raid. Look how dangerous that could be. We would be much safer with the girls of Liverpool or Southport. Our mothers would be pleased about that.

With tongue in cheek, we took this problem to our Jaunty. He eyed us for a long time; he even walked round us twice. Then, to our surprise, he nodded.

"After last night, you may well be right. Where will you stay?"

"Oh, Salvation Army, YMCA. We'll find somewhere." We hardly dared breathe.

"All right, you've got all night leave," nodded our Jaunty. "You be back on board by 0800. And keep out of trouble."

That was when we decided that we would shave every morning from then on whether we needed it or not.

As we walked out of the railway station in Southport it felt almost like coming home. We soon learnt there was no Hoe, but there was a pier and a magnificent marine lake with boats. We loved Southport from the moment we saw it. Just outside the station was a cafe that we made our own, and the ladies who worked there went out of their way to see we had the best of everything. When they heard we were going to stay somewhere tonight they wanted to know where. Fred and me felt they were going to keep us on the straight and narrow no matter what ideas we might have had. One of them gave us a card.

"Mrs Jones," she said. "It's the big house at the end of the street there. Tell her we sent you."

We had to sleep somewhere, and while this was not as exciting as the ideas we had started out with, it would be a good base to start from.

Mrs Jones seemed pleased to see us. She showed us to a huge room with four beds in it, gave us a key to the front door and told us she would call us at six in the morning in time for breakfast and the early train back to Liverpool.

I had Lorna's address and fully intended to call at the house, but as we passed in front of the station I saw the most wonderful girl sitting alone on a seat near the gate to the platform. Fred saw her as well and she drew us both into the building like two pins on a sheet being moved by a magnet under it. Her hair was shoulder length, blonde, but even to us, seemed to be lighter than blonde. There were slight shadows beneath her eyes as she stared at us apprehensively, she pulled a woollen scarf closer around her shoulders.

We were much nearer before we noticed the blanket over her knees and neither Fred or me saw the older man and woman with the wheelchair until they stopped by our side. The woman nodded to us, waiting for us to turn away, and there was a resigned look about the lovely girl on the seat in front of us.

Fred, never before known for his diplomacy, was suddenly

gentle as he asked "Can you walk without that?" He had his hand on the wheelchair.

She shook her head and a tear slanted across her cheek. Fred looked at me, and I was startled to see anger smouldering in his eyes. I knew exactly what he had in mind and forestalled him. Turning to the older couple, I asked "Can we borrow her?"

They hesitated, looking at each other. "We were just going home, waiting for the train."

"Catch a later one," urged Fred, more eager than I had ever seen him. "We'll bring her back here to you."

The girl on the bench seemed to come alive. The older couple could see the difference for themselves. They looked carefully at us, then the woman suddenly smiled. "Take good care of her", she said, and pushed the chair at us.

Taking an arm each as her worried parents stepped aside, she felt as light as a feather as we lifted her into her chair and tucked in the blanket. With a whoop of warning to the startled travellers Fred raced out of the station without waiting for me. I caught up with him further along Lord Street and slowed him down a bit. Fred seemed happier than I had seen him before, and there was no doubt in my mind that he was not doing this just for a girl in a wheelchair.

"Fred, let's look for Lorna. Perhaps she'll join us."

Fred shook his head, "You look for her, I'm taking Kitty to the lake."

Kitty. So that was her name. She was pretty, just like her name. I held out my hand, "Hello Kit."

She laughed up at me, but her small hand was cold. In the daylight away from the shadows of the station the dark hollows under her eyes were more pronounced. Whatever excitement we might have to offer seemed to me to be running out of time.

I grinned back at her, knowing that I wasn't in the way. "The lake it is. Let's go."

It turned out to be a mad afternoon. She shrieked as loudly as any of us as the little sail boat flapped its way around. We demonstrated quite clearly that though we might be hot stuff at steering warships, we were not much good at sailing small boats. From the lake to the pier, to the cafe, then to the theatre and finally, with little time to spare, we raced her wheelchair back to the station, where her parents were waiting on the same seat where we had started from, though I suppose they had not been far behind us all day. In all fairness, we had not seen them.

I kissed her cheek and gently tapped her chin with my fist before moving away and leaving her with Fred. I shook hands with her parents and took them away, or was it they who took me away?

The man looked at his watch. "I'll have to break it up," he said reluctantly. "I don't want to, not now, but we'll miss our train."

We looked across the station to Fred and Kitty. He was kneeling on the floor in front of her chair and they were holding hands as they talked. I remember thinking it would leave marks on the knees of his uniform. She gave him something that he looked at, then put away in his pocket. Then he kissed her. It was not the peck like I had given her, but a real hug. And she was kissing him back, with her arms around his neck, holding tight. At last she released him, and he stood up. I watched her parents wheel her away and lifted my hand in salute as they went through the gate onto the platform.

Fred was coming towards me and there were white patches on his knees. His eyes were suspiciously bright and he blew his nose rather frequently. Our cafe was still open and we went in for coffee.

"You all right, Fred?" I asked, trying not to stare at him too hard. I thought I had given him enough time to recover. After all, we had only met her that afternoon; he had only known her a few hours.

"Sure," he replied, much too quickly.

I looked at him over the rim of my coffee cup. "We'll find her again, next time we're back here in Southport."

"We'll be lucky," he muttered. "She was just out for the day from the hospital. She gave me this." He took a little silver cross and chain from his pocket to show me, then pocketed it as he got up and walked out.

We made our way back towards our digs through quiet and empty streets.

"Look," said Fred suddenly, pointing. Far away in the dark sky in the direction of Liverpool there were twinkling lights just like a far away firework display. Our Liverpool was being beaten up again. We stood and watched for a while, until a red glow began etching the rooftops and chimneys of Southport. Even to two young men, with money to spare, out together for a night on the town, it seemed insane to have to watch a city burn. To what depths would we have to sink before we could come out of this nightmare. Would a lovely girl like Kitty ever see the lights come on again. Would we?

Suddenly cold, I shivered, "Let's get drunk!"

Fred grunted, "Trust you! The pub's shut an hour ago. Next time, though." He left his threat unvoiced.

On the train back to Exchange station next morning, the white patches on Fred's knees were still visible in spite of both our efforts to remove them. There could not have been much sleep for anyone in the city during the night, but men were working everywhere, clearing away rubble from the roads, making damaged buildings safe. Ships were moving in the docks, and we acquired another armful of big oranges as we passed the unloading quay.

It was 0750 as we crossed the gangway and our Jaunty was waiting for us with our cards in his hand just like a worried father watching for the return of his daughters. He was more relieved to see us than we were to see him.

"Staggering back from your night of love and passion, eh?" he greeted us. "Been licking it!" He was pointing to the white marks on Fred's knees.

Both of us, too innocent at that age to know what he meant, stared at him. "No", said Fred, exposing himself for the knockout, "I was kneeling on a platform."

The Jaunty's eyes opened wide. "She was too tall for you?"

Only then did Fred understand what he was talking about. As his face darkened with anger I shouldered him aside, and the oranges he was holding fell to the deck. We gathered them up and went below to Two mess, right forward on the port side which was the seaman's mess deck. Quickly we changed into overalls and the happenings of last night became just a memory.

Chapter Five

Feeling guilty about Lorna, I decided I would write to her new address and arrange to meet her at the railway station we were coming to know so well, only to have my letter sent back from the ship's office. How dare I tell a girl friend that HMS *Wellington* was in Liverpool? Hitler might read it. Did I want to lose the war?

No use protesting that I hadn't said the *Wellington* was in Liverpool, all I said was that I would meet her in Southport.

"There's no docks in Southport, is there? Where d'you think that Hitler will assume the *Wellington* is lurking?"

Suitably impressed about the importance of HMS *Wellington*, I wondered how the heck I was ever going to make contact with my lovely, bathing suit clad Lorna. With my overalls getting too small for me by the minute, I was breathless at the thought of that lithe body twisting out of my grasp off Plymouth Hoe leaving her bathing suit in my hands.

"You're dribbling!" stated Fred.

I came back to the present with a start. "No, I'm not," I denied, wiping my chin. "Just can't wait to get back to Southport. Next time ashore?"

"Sure", replied Fred, but not quite so eagerly. "Why not?"

Fate seemed to be all against us, between the air raids, fires, and dockside damage, the watch on leave were coming back to the ship all too soon with lighter suitcases, except for our Irish colleagues, who were staggering back with laden cases that emptied out on the mess tables piles of butter and boxes of eggs to swell our rations. So startled were we to see such unrationed foodstuffs that we almost forgot to insult them over the civvies they were wearing.

They came back to a *Wellington* that looked different. Every time in harbour something was added or taken away. Within hours of their return, cranes were swinging out the welding sets, lines of lorries had been emptied and were moving away.

Soon it was evening time, and out in the river many ships were moving down channel. In Gladstone Dock, smoke was issuing from several of the escort's funnels. Wires had been singled up, gangways had gone. Dockyard workmen stood on the quay and watched. Some papers, orange wrappers no doubt, swirled round and round in the wind eddies near the remains of a burnt out warehouse. Orders were shouted, telegraph bells clanged. Wires splashed into the water as they were let go. Water swirled white and foaming under the sterns of the ships as one after the other they lined up for the dock entrance.

When the lock gate opened, it was remarkable how quickly they gained speed, but the warning air raid sirens were blasting as we reeled up our wires. Even before we gained the river, incendiary bombs were falling on New Brighton. We could see them sprinkling across the fair ground buildings. Fires began starting everywhere we looked. In the dusk of the evening, and by the glow of the fires, we could see men running to put them out.

We stood on the deck with fists clenched and tight lips as we jockeyed for position in the lines of ships moving towards the sea. Behind us in the dark there were the familiar flashes of the bombs, and that awesome red glow of spreading fires. The sky above Liverpool was a sprinkling mass of giant starlights as the city defences hit back.

Turning left and passing south, but well out of sight of Southern Ireland, our huge convoy was making for Gibraltar, and on towards Africa.

After every spell in harbour, most of us were seasick for the first few hours. We pretended not to be, but it happened to most. Until the beer and the greasy chips had been spewed up in the secrecy of the toilets, or Heads, as they were called, we all felt queezy at the motion of the ship. But once it was up, we would be as right as rain. As soon as possible after leaving, hoses would be unreeled and decks washed down to get rid of the dirt of the land.

Everyone wanted to shower and change their underclothes, as if the very smell of the land must be washed away. With so many men living so close together in such small spaces, it had to be like that. Woe betide anyone who walked around with the slightest mark on his underclothes. Once, a chap took his shirt off, and his singlet was a shade yellow with age. Everyone in the mess cowered away from him until he took it off and threw it overboard. We could buy new underclothes from the ship's stores, so there was no excuse for looking shabby.

Most of us had a small allotment from our pay to Bernards, the Naval tailors. They had shops at all our Naval bases. All we had to do was walk in and get measured for a new uniform suit, and it would be ready to collect a couple of days later. All other items of uniform could be selected from them, so we had no problem in keeping our kit smart and new.

With over a hundred men all living in close proximity there had to be plenty of scrubbing and cleaning. We had a bathroom, but with no bath, just a tiled space next to the Heads. A bath was a shower, or bucket of water tipped over your head. There was no privacy, and you soon got used to walking about naked, carrying your towel.

A favourite pastime was for everyone you met while on your way from the bathroom to your mess, to stop and stare. Then they would follow you, and it usually ended with the victim running for dear life with everyone he passed grabbing for his belongings.

There was one chap we called the Duchess. I think he was one of our sparkers, that is telegraphists. He rigged up a screen in the corner of our bathroom to hide behind while he washed. Everyone who came in stared at this unusual sight, then naturally pulled the screen aside to see what was going on, only to be confronted by the Duchess cowering naked behind it. He didn't keep this up for long, and was soon walking naked as happily as the rest of us. We washed our clothes in a bucket with soap flakes, or whatever we could get from our NAAFI shop. We were lucky to have a small drying room above the boilers. It would dry our washing within an hour. But we wouldn't dare go in there without our shoes on! There was a space under the ladder to the upper deck near the Jaunty's office where we could hang our oilskins and other wet clothes when coming down off watch to save taking them on to the mess deck.

From the shelter of B gun, we looked at the Leading Seaman of the Watch as the telephone on the quarterdeck wailed. The faster you turned the handle on the telephone, the higher the wail sounded. This didn't sound like a furious wail. We looked down at him as he answered it.

"You're wanted on the bridge". He was looking at me. I hadn't done anything. Puzzled, I made my way forward. On the bridge I was told we were passing through an area where a ship had been torpedoed a few days ago. There may be survivors. "D'you want to volunteer?"

I smiled grimly to myself. Volunteer!

They phoned the masthead, and he was coming down before I left the shelter of the bridge. Climbing the mast was second nature to me now, and I sat on the yard-arm above the crow's nest. Spots of rain were tapping on my oilskins, and I pulled the rim of my sou'wester down over my eyes. The *Wellington* was out on the starboard side of the convoy, zig-zagging quietly, so we were covering an area that no one else would see. I had been up there for well over an hour, and was getting a bit cold when I felt a movement to the side of the mast. Looking down, someone was shaking one of the wire stays, and when they saw me looking, waved for me to come down. I waved back. Right. I stood up, arms round the mast, and took a last, long, careful look around, and came to rest on nothing.

Down on the bridge, everyone seemed to be peering with their binoculars along the line I had seemed interested in, but if I couldn't see anything from up there, they wouldn't. Still, I felt uneasy. It must have been something that had caught my attention.

I slipped down over the yard-arm into the crow's nest and turned the handle of the telephone. "Can we go out thataway a bit, Sir, just to make sure?" I held out my arm in the direction I wanted to go.

I felt the speed increasing by the way the mast began to lay back as her bows lifted. Back up on the yard-arm it was more difficult to hold on now because of her livelier motion.

After a while the loud hailer on the bridge called to me. "We're getting a bit far from the convoy." I looked around. Indeed we were, they were almost out of sight. But I had my target. I was looking at something way out there ahead of us. But for the life of me, I couldn't decide what it was.

I looked down at the bridge. All faces were turned my way. Not only on the bridge, but along the upper deck as well. I put my thumb up, and pointed ahead. All binoculars on the ship were searching now, but it would be another twenty minutes or so before anybody down there would see it.

Arms held firmly around the mast, I stared at the tiny black dot, there were two of them now. Through cupped hands, I shouted down. "Open lifeboats, two of them".

Shivering with cold, but feeling well pleased with my afternoon's work, I made sure there was nothing else to see, then slipped over the yard-arm to the ladder, and climbed down.

Back aft on the low quarterdeck the scrambling nets were being cut loose. We craned over the guard rails, staring ahead at the two big lifeboats we were rapidly coming up on.

At first it seemed there was no one in them, then dark faces began looking over the gunwhales at us. Then there were shouts and wild waving. They hadn't seen us until then. As we slid alongside them, members of our crew who were hanging on the nets dropped into the boats to hold them and help the survivors. They all seemed too weak to help themselves, but everyone stopped dead in their tracks when we saw the Captain and First Mate tied up in the stern of the boat. No one moved until we had cut them free and lifted them up to the deck where the First Aid party was waiting. Then the boats were emptied, and sunk with gunfire. Within minutes, the scrambling nets were being recovered and the *Wellington* was heading back at full speed for the convoy.

Picking up survivors from a torpedoed ship.

The *Wellington* was fortunate in that we carried a doctor, and as things were to turn out, so was I. To help him, we had a Leading Sick Bay Artisifer, a hard working chap who wore bulging spectacles, known affectionately to all of us as Doc. I remember those two with gratitude.

There was a small, two bed sick bay, on one side of the Stokers' mess deck, and for the rest of the voyage to Gibraltar it was overworked as they cared for the people we had saved. The Captain and First Mate were the worst off; They had tried to ration the water from the first night they were adrift, and had been overpowered and tied up.

The authorities at Gib would have to deal with that when we handed them over.

That evening we all gathered on the Stokers mess deck in response to a pipe that we had never heard before. "Tombola will be played on the Stokers mess deck at 1700."

"What's tombola?" we asked. Only the older hands knew, and all they would say was, "Get your money ready."

That was the first time we had ever heard of, or played, bingo. It was organised by two of our Leading Seamen, who sold the tickets, and one of them pulled numbers out of a bag and placed them on a board. Whenever the weather was reasonable we played tombola twice a week from then on.

It was on one of these Gibraltar bound trips that I reached that wonderful milestone that comes to everyone, their twenty-first birthday. Class 178 from Training Division were all about the same age, so twenty-first birthdays were quite common about then.

Everyone who drew their tot of rum dutifully presented me with their tot for the first sip, as was my right. I wasn't a man yet in the eyes of the Navy, I wasn't allowed a tot of my own, at least, not until today. But from today I could draw my own tot, and stay out all night as well if I wanted to. Those nights of love and passion we had been waiting for were here. Look out girls, we're ready! Fat lot of good that was going to be to us right now.

I had the afternoon watch that day, and my first trick was on the wheel. The Quartermaster had his doubts about letting me get my hands on his spokes, but as I was still standing at that stage, he sat with the Duty Petty Officer of the Watch near the rev counter, probably discussing where to hide me when the collapse came. Petty Officer Macmillan, Mac to all of us, was from the Hebrides, and he was a great seaman. He taught me splices and sennets that would stand me in good stead when I would reach his rank.

They didn't have long to wait. I was struggling to keep her on her course, and if you turned the wheel too fast it caused the steering engine back in the tiller flat to vibrate the ship as it tried to keep up with the demand. The Chief Engineer would feel that, and he would come haring up the ladder from below to play hell with us for mistreating his engines.

Out of the voice pipe near my ear came a roar of rage from the bridge above. "Quartermaster! You're writing your name in the bloody wake!"

I was quietly manoeuvred into the space in front of the binnacle and covered with a spare Union Jack like a corpse waiting for burial. I didn't even hear the angry Engineer Officer berating the Quartermaster.

Gibraltar. We stared wide-eyed at the white fortress towering above us as we stood motionless along the forecastle, with spotless shirts and shorts fluttering in the gentle breeze on a warm and cloudless morning. We steamed into harbour and made for our berth on the mole. After three weeks at sea it felt as if the mole was moving. It was a quick change back into overalls after the entering harbour routine, and there was the usual flurry of activity of stores and supplies.

After dinner, in our best white suits, we fell in on the boat deck for inspection before going ashore. "Remember," we were warned, "this is a fortress, there are more of them than you. Behave yourselves."

We walked up Main Street with rising excitement. The shops were full of unrationed sweets and chocolates, cigarettes and tobacco, silk stockings and dressing gowns, all the things that had long since disappeared from the shops at home. There were silks and scents, lipsticks and lace, watches and wines, bags and bangles. I could see Lorna slinking down the stairs, clad in one of the silk dressing gowns I was going to buy, silk stockings peeping from beneath it, rattling her bangles. I couldn't afford a bra, so she wouldn't be we . . .

"You're dribbling again," accused Fred.

I started, wiping my chin. "No, I'm not."

The sound of a band drew us across the street to the wide open doors of a bar. At the end of a long, well filled room, on a small platform, were a group of ladies playing the most beautiful music we ever heard. On an easel beside them it informed us that we were listening to Ivy Benson and her all girls band. On a large notice above the bar it stated that all drinks in this establishment will be free on Victory Day.

In no time at all we were seated at one of the tables with foaming pints in front of us. I casually brushed a fly off my bare knee, while Fred winced as he eased a stuck, sweaty leg from the seat of his chair.

"Cor! This is the life," murmured Fred, stretching his legs out. "There must be easier ways of earning a living than the way we are doing it." Suddenly he sat up. "Look."

Standing on the pavement outside in the hot sun, glaring in at us, was one of our Leading Seamen from the ship. Four of our shipmates, waiting on the road, stared at us enviously. They were all immaculately dressed in white suits, with white belts and gaiters. The shore patrol.

Every ship had to put patrols ashore to keep over-boisterous crews in order. Normally, the very sight of a patrol would have us taking hands out of pockets, squaring shoulders, putting caps on straight. Especially if the patrol was from another ship. But with your own, you would take liberties.

We grabbed our pints and rushed to the door, licked our lips, and made all sorts of appreciative noises as we tormented our sweaty mates outside until they marched off up the street.

Being men didn't feel any different from being boys. There was no all night leave in Gib. There were no women there either except the Rock Scorpions (the locals), and if you dared smile at those you were liable to be hit over the head with whatever they were carrying at the time.

With all the silks, scents, and stockings that we could afford, we watched a play in the Garrick theatre, then back to Ivy's for the remainder of the evening. There we saw white coated figures with baskets strapped to them selling prawns, with salt and vinegar available in the basket. Others were selling whole, roasted chickens.

We had never seen anything like that before, chickens being a once a year treat at Christmas. Suddenly hungry, we had a whole chicken between us, though I must admit it wasn't as big as the ones we used to have at home.

Ivy's girls belted out the music, and the pints came and went as others from our ship joined us. Two sailors came in sporting massive beards, looking like someone from the Bible about to part the Red Sea. We didn't know them, so made no room for them at our table. They stood there, hairy and menacing, just glaring, as conspicuous as a lamp post in a blackout. And Fred had to start bleating like a goat.

The reaction was instant. A fist shot out at him. He moved his face aside just in time but was knocked over the table by the wind of it. I kicked old Hairy's feet from under him, just as Jonesy, one of our Leading Seamen, yanked the beard of the other one.

There were pools of beer and broken glasses on the floor, the band was screaming, a roasted chicken took off for the door as if it was still alive, and our patrol came running in from outside.

We all drew together like insulted females, pointing accusingly at the two unfortunate men who were hopping and gasping among the broken glasses. Without even a warning glance, our patrol grabbed them and marched out, and as soon as it was safe to do so, we followed, back towards the ship.

The lights of the shops and the street, the windows and the floodlit gardens took our breath away. Our upside down world seemed suddenly normal, just as we remembered it. Safely back on board the *Wellington*, we stood on the upper deck in the warm and still night, staring at the lights of the Rock towering above us, and the shimmer of those far away at La Linea in Spain, and Tangiers, across the Straights in Morocco.

From below on the mess deck came a roar of laughter, and not wanting to miss anything, we hurried below to see what was going on. One of our older men, bleary eyed and happy, was propped up on the table giving one of the Navy's well know recitations. You know the sort.

In the Street of a Thousand . . . Beneath the Sign of the . . . I can't write it here or I'd get arrested.

This time he was telling the tale about the Jaunty who dreamt he was dead, and was walking with the Devil through a big hall with boiling vats all along the side. He lifts up the lid of the first vat, and Jimmy the One (First Lieutenant) comes moaning up with the steam. He hastily slams the lid, and walks on to the next vat. There are many vats, and each one holds a recognisable figure from your ship. All of this would be in verse.

While we had been ashore the mail had caught up with us, and among the many birthday cards from home was one from the girl across the street. It had the picture of a race-course on it, with the words, *They're Off.* Inside the card, when you opened it, was a tiny pair of cotton knickers.

All too soon we were preparing for sea, our last letters had been posted in the ship's postbox. It would be three weeks before we would be able to write again. Babies would be born, people could die, homes could be destroyed. It would be three weeks before we would know about it.

Two days out of Gib, with the *Wellington* zig-zagging at the head of a large homeward bound convoy, I was finding difficulty in breathing. I didn't want any dinner, and spent the dinner hour asleep on the lockers. I had even given away my tot.

Fred offered to do the afternoon watch for me, but he would have to do his own watch after, so I couldn't let him do that. With my first trick on the wheel, I sat on a stool, trying to see the compass, struggling for breath.

The Quartermaster took the wheel, and I was helped down to the sick bay.

Doc stared at me through his bulging glasses. "I'll get the quack."

There were no miracle drugs to fight pneumonia in those days. Our Quack and Doc did it. Every day, someone from my mess brought in a dinner for me, and every day they had to take it back and share it between the others. After the first week, they decided they would wait for Doc to tell them if I wanted anything to eat.

The same thing happened to my tot, until one day I was conscious enough to understand what Doc was protesting about.

"For Christ sake, take it," he said. "You don't have to drink it. I'll do that."

From then on, with a shaky hand, I accepted the tot without noting the look of disappointment on the face of the one that brought it to me, and left it on the locker by my bed. I never saw Doc drink it, but when he did, it was a very small reward indeed for what he was doing for me.

We were nearly home before I became fully aware of what was going on. When I first saw myself in the sick bay mirror it nearly frightened me to death. I hadn't shaved for three weeks, and patches of downy hair stuck out at odd places. If that was what I would look like with a beard, I was glad I hadn't requested to be allowed to grow one. With my thin and sunken cheeks I looked more like a goat than a goat did.

After leaving the convoy in the Irish Sea, a thrill of excitement went round the ship. The *Wellington* was due for a refit. Months of constant sea time had taken their toll. There was a long list of defects getting longer with every voyage. There were new types of guns and other weapons being developed. New radio equipment available. She needed protection against magnetic mines, and her speed was being reduced by weeds growing on the bottom below the water line.

A refit! Dry docking. New weapons, new everything. This could take two months. Two months in harbour. Shore leave, being able to make dates. Day after tomorrow, under the clock. You bet, yes, we'll be there. Home leave, three weeks each perhaps?

But where would it be? What port would they send us to. Plymouth? Liverpool? Greenock, or Gourock? Rumour was rife. The strongest one was that we would all be sent back to Plymouth for drafting to other ships, and a new crew would take over the *Wellington* when she was ready for sea again.

No one fancied that last one. You can become very attached to a ship and to the people who serve in it. Better the devil you know, sort of thing. Then came the word. Rumour had been laid. She would always be our ship. We would be refitting at a place called Sheerness, but stopping briefly at the Naval base at Chatham first. There would be three weeks home leave for each watch.

After so much time at sea, every man aboard would have a suitcase full of packets of cigarettes saved up by now. We could buy these from our NAAFI canteen on the ship. We could also buy half pound tins of tobacco from the ship's store, and while at sea we would smoke our own rolled cigarettes and save the packeted ones. All of this was duty free, and much cheaper for us to buy on the ship than it was ashore, even when you could get them. For a day's shore leave, we could take two packets with us, but when going on leave, eight packets were the limit.

By the time we arrived at Chatham, I was just about able to walk around the sick bay, but hadn't started eating yet. Doc came struggling in with a very heavy looking suit case.

"Get back into bed!" he snapped. "The ambulance will be here for you in a minute."

Before I could strangle him, the doctor came in. He waved my pleadings firmly away. "I can't help spoiling your leave, but if you went down with T.B. in later life you wouldn't thank me any. No. It's to hospital for you."

Doc was positively beaming behind his thick glasses. He was too far away for me to kick him on his ankle, but he was obviously pleased about something.

Not long afterwards, they loaded me onto a stretcher. Friends pulled my hair, shook hands, wished me luck, and I was carried ashore to a waiting Naval ambulance.

Doc got in with us, struggling now with two suitcases.

He looked at me anxiously as I slowly began to smile. All my kit was here with me in the ambulance. Suitcase, kit bag, hammock, hat box, attache case. Distributed amongst it was all the silks and scents from Gib, pounds of tobacco, and many packets of cigarettes.

Doc slid his heavy case under the stretcher, and the other one went beneath the pillow under my head.

I wasn't doing anything wrong. I was being taken from one duty free zone to another. Doc seemed to be sweating though, and his glasses kept steaming up.

We went through the dockyard, passing many ships, crossing railway lines, under cranes, and to the dockyard gates, where we came to a halt outside the police office. The ambulance doors opened and two faces looked in at us. I opened my mouth to say something, and Doc stuck his dirty hanky into it.

"I've got a very sick man in here," he declared, as I choked, staring at them through his thick glasses.

They slammed the doors without saying a word, and the ambulance moved on. I lashed out at Doc, but he was out of range again.

"You wouldn't hit a man with glasses?" he grinned, taking them off to wipe away the steam, then he banged on the window behind the driver. They stopped to let him off in the town, and even helped to unload his suitcases. He was standing on the pavement waving as the doors closed. I managed to toss his dirty handkerchief after him. It felt just as if someone had turned out the light. I was alone, in a strange place, among strangers. I missed my friends, I missed my ship, and I wasn't feeling very well.

They treated me there at the hospital for three weeks. I slept a lot, thankful that pneumonia had caused me no lasting harm. There were visitors to most of the patients each evening, and some would come and talk to me if I was awake. But they were strangers, and we would soon run out of things to talk about. So mostly at visiting times I would pretend to be asleep, thinking with closed eyes about Fred, Doc, Jonesy, and the others, and more often than not, I would fall fast asleep and wake long after visiting time was over. There was such an awful lot of sleep to catch up on.

I heard my name being whispered, and thought it was a dream. Then I heard it again, and someone touched my face. I opened my eyes and stared at her, she was only inches away.

I was dreaming, of course. I closed my eyes again.

"Wake up, silly." She pulled my ear.

I sat up, unable to believe my eyes. Susan, the girl across the street. From the other side of the world, a lifetime away. We had fought tooth and nail as kids, played doctors and nurses, kissed behind the bicycle shed, fell in the river, met different friends, went our own way, met and talked on the pavement. I had stopped once or twice to look after her as she passed. She was just the girl from across the street, you never really see them.

But I was seeing her now. Her large, brown eyes were searching my face with concern. White teeth were biting her lower lip that was within inches of mine, and getting closer all the time as I leaned towards her.

"You're a long way from being dead," she laughed as she pushed me away. "Your mother was worried sick about you. She asked me to call and have a look at you."

"And you came here all the way from Wales?"

She shook her head. "I'm working in Croydon. It's not too far."

"Can you get back there tonight?"

She looked at me with a slow smile lighting her face. Her red lips were close to mine, and were very inviting. "Of course not. I'm sleeping with you. Move up!"

I chuckled. "You haven't seen our sister. She's probably having kittens right now at the thought of the damage you're doing to me."

"What damage?" She was suddenly concerned.

I couldn't help but notice those swellings under her navy blue sweater. Had I been a blind fool all these years, I wondered?

"After they take my blood pressure tonight they'll have me in an oxygen tent. But where are you staying? This is a Navy town, you know what sailors are like." I tried to hide it with a laugh, but I was suddenly very jealous.

"At the YWCA. It's near the station. I called there before I came on here. I go home every weekend, I'll tell your mum I saw you."

I nodded glumly. Just my luck. A man at last, and here was a lovely girl, within reach, available all night, and me, too blasted weak to get out of bed. I had written home as soon as I knew where I was.

The bell to end visiting hour was ringing. It seemed a much shorter time than usual. We held hands tightly, her face was very close to mine.

"You're very thin," she whispered. "What have they been doing to you?" She didn't look at all like the ragamuffin that I used to climb trees with. I wanted to hold her and squeeze her to me, but didn't dare.

"It's these nurses," I gulped, hardly able to talk. "We have orgies here every night. Takes it out of you."

"Time please." Sister was calling.

"Will you come again? I was still holding tight to her hands.

"Yes, if you will still be here. Think you will?"

I shook my head. "Dunno, better leave it. See you at home. Take care."

"And you." She kissed me, and brushed away a tear from her cheek. "And eat something, damn you!"

I watched her walk away from me along the ward, and wished with all my heart that I could have gone with her. She turned at the door to look back, lifted her hand in farewell. I was left staring at an empty doorway, and thinking of all the chances I had let slip by. It was much later when I remembered the birthday card she had sent. *They're Off.* I would be stronger the next time we met, I promised myself.

Chapter Six

Two weeks later I was discharged to the Naval barracks at Chatham with instructions to be sent home on three weeks' sick leave, so I wasn't going to lose my refitting leave after all. An ambulance took me from the hospital to the barracks, complete with all my kit, including Gibraltar silks and scents, cigarettes, and tins of tobacco.

All of this was safely locked in the baggage store, and I went out of the gates with my regulation eight packets of cigarettes, in a uniform that felt much too big for me.

It was no use protesting to mother that the Navy had declared her son to be a man. I was hauled protectively into her ample bosom, and fed on the best that wartime rations would allow. I quickly began to fill my uniform again. And then on Friday night, Sue came home.

I met her on the platform of our local station. As she stepped off the train I halted almost in mid word as a hefty chap in civilian clothes got off with her and took her small case.

She eyed me quizzically as I hesitated to speak. There was a little half smile around her mouth as she indicated her companion.

"This is Tom. He's a coal miner. I told you about him."

I thought desperately. Had she, heck! But she obviously wanted him to think so, so who was I to spoil anything for her? A coal miner. Reserved occupation. He would always be on hand whenever she was home. Not like me.

I nodded to Tom, and held out my hand. We shook hands, and it was like holding a wet fish. I almost shuddered at the thought of that kind of hand slipping over those lovely swellings that even now were making me feel breathless.

"You look much better than the last time I saw you," she said, as we all walked out of the station, and I gritted my teeth as I saw Tom take her arm in an obvious gesture of ownership. A slight frown of irritation crossed her face, but she didn't shake him off. As if she thought some kind of explanation was due, she said, "I've known Tom for nearly a year now." There was no trace of regret in the way she looked at me, and I was the only one to blame. I had blown my chances many times.

We were passing the Station Hotel, and I felt the need to escape. "I've promised to meet someone in here," I blurted out, and took a couple of steps towards the door.

Tom hardly checked his pace, glad to be rid of a nuisance, but Sue stopped, looking very hard at me. "You could kiss me," she stated, slightly hurt. "I'm not married to him."

I pecked her on the cheek, smelling her perfume. Before either of us could say anything more, Tom was walking on, almost pulling her with him. All the thoughts that were bubbling inside me seemed suddenly out of place. Her birthday card, locked up in the barrack store at Chatham with my possessions, had better stay safely locked away. These were mad times, and the thoughts that I had been entertaining had no place in them. I stumbled into the hotel, and stayed there until I felt safe to come out.

I did not see Sue again. She cut short her weekend at home, and went back to Croydon the next morning.

All too soon my sick leave was over, and it was off to this strange place called Chatham. It took a long time to find my belongings, as a lot of kit had been loaded into and taken out of that baggage store since the last time I saw it.

A fat Chief Petty Officer behind the window of the drafting office had never heard of the *Wellington*, or of me. "You belong here now," he told me. "You're due a spell ashore, anyway. Make yourself at home."

I walked round that barracks like a lost soul. I knew no one, and no one seemed to want to know me. That evening I took a bus to Sheerness, and recognised the familiar mast poking above one of the buildings. Soon, I was standing on the edge of a dry dock, looking at the *Wellington* sitting on a long line of chocks and propped upright with huge baulks of timber wedged between the dock walls and her sides, just as she was when I had first seen her long ago back there in Cardiff. Stages were hanging along her sides, and blue welding flashes were coming from below and along her decks.

I crossed the gangway and made my way forward to the seaman's mess deck amid many shouts of welcome. It was great to taste the strong tea again with Ideal milk. Unusually, there was plenty of sugar in the cupboard, a sure sign there had been no night watchkeeping.

In the ship's office, I explained that I was just a number in Chatham barracks.

"You are still on our books," I was told. "You've got to come back. We'll get on to them in the morning."

Feeling very relieved, I invited myself to supper, and did not in the least feel guilty about eating their rations while mine was probably going to waste back in the barracks.

I caught the bus back to Chatham late that night, and looked with regret at the YWCA near the station as I passed. After a drink in the NAAFI canteen in the barracks, I spent the night on a settee in one of the messes, as I hadn't yet found a place to sling my hammock.

Next morning, just after breakfast, sure enough, there was a tannoy message calling my name, "Report to the drafting office."

The same fat Chief Petty Officer looked at me from behind the window. If he recognised me, he gave no sign of it. He was probably a Naval pensioner called up from the reserve, with a home and family right here in Chatham.

He thrust some papers out at me. "Be on Pier Head by 1100, you're on draft to something called the *Wellington*." He slammed the window down hard. I had interrupted his tea.

I was sitting on my hammock with the rest of my kit nearby long before 1100. A trot boat collected me from the Pier and took me down to Sheerness. I was landed at some steps just a stone's throw away from the *Wellington* sitting there in her dry dock.

I had rejoined just as the second half of her crew were returning from leave. The ship seemed to be in more of a mess that when we had first seen her in Cardiff. The washrooms and heads were roped off, as you could hardly flush a loo full of jollop out through a pipe in the ship's bottom and perhaps all over some workmen who would be welding something underneath her below in the dry dock. We had to use the toilet facilities provided on the dock side.

The fire in the galley was working though, and a tank full of water was always boiling ready to make tea whenever anyone felt like making some. The sink in the corner of the galley could not be used either, as dirty hot washing up water was just as unacceptable as a lavatory full of other stuff.

Next day, with shore leave piped from 1200, Fred and I decided to explore Sheerness, and on the Promenade we met Margery and Edith. It was the easiest meeting we had so far managed. Fred was being attacked by a bulldog that looked just like Winston Churchill, while I stood on a seat and yelled at it to go away. A girl ran up and scolded it, and it just slunk off.

"It's a nuisance," she told us. "It does that to everyone. It's from that house over there. Did he bite you?"

'Yes," lied Fred, limping. "Look out! He's coming again." He put his arms round her as if to protect her.

Believing him, I leapt back on the seat again, and nearly fell over Edith, who was already up there.

Edith's mother must have been married to a Jaunty. She was all right as long as she could see my hands, but every time I went to reach for something in my pocket she jumped two yards sideways. She must have had her doubts about Fred too, every time he turned towards her she managed to be three feet away from him.

At first it was a game. Fred or me would move our hands, and we would grin at each other as Edith jumped. He soon got on better terms with Marge. She didn't seem to mind as he put his arm around her waist as we walked along the Prom, and when his arm slipped down she put up with it until someone else came near. I tried that with Edith, but she must have had something very valuable that she wasn't going to let me get my hands on. We walked very sedately along that prom, with me jealously eyeing the rear of the pair in front. Edith softened a little as the afternoon went by, and once, as we all sat on a wall together, she even went so far as to put her arm in mine.

It was dark when we got out of the cinema, and the girl I was with seemed intent on keeping the same regulation distance from me. We were men now, or so the Navy reluctantly agreed. We didn't have to be back safely under the eye of our Jaunty by 2300, we could stay out all night if we wanted to. The nights of passion that we had so looked forward to was a long time in coming, and the thought of going to bed with Edith, with my hands stuck up in the air all night caused me to chuckle out loud, and Edith looked at me suspiciously.

Fred precipitated what followed, no doubt encouraged by the way Margery was clinging to him. He looked at me pointedly. "Marge and me are going in there," he said, indicating a dark looking back lane behind the cinema. "Where are you going?"

I hadn't thought about it and was taken by surprise, I answered hesitantly, "We'll go in the other end of it." I reached for Edith's arm, expecting her to hare off up the road at any second, and even Fred stepped aside to make way for her to pass. But no. She came with me, and we left Fred and Marge standing on the pavement.

It was very dark in the lane, and I nearly fell over a bucket or something as we walked along. We stopped near a gateway, and I found she was as warm as toast under her coat. I was thinking that if only she had given me some of the encouragement earlier in the day as she was giving me now I would have had a much more exciting time.

I undid some buttons, and silently cussed the clot who had invented those fearsome metal catches on a bra. I felt her face lift to mine as I gave up, there was no need to undo it, you could get round that. Then we heard a commotion down the lane away. Somebody fell over the same bucket that I had, and we hastily put ourselves decent just as Fred blundered into us.

"She hit me," he protested, "right in the mush!"

"So will I," I snarled. "Go away!" I turned back to Edith, reaching for where I had left off. She pushed me away.

"Where's Marge?" she asked him. "What did you do to her?"

"Nothing," protested Fred. "She's out there on the pavement."

Edith hurried off, and I kicked the wall in temper as she went, leaving me with feelings that would take a long time to subside. We hurried out of the lane after the girls, but there was no sign of them.

I stared coldly at Fred, who was shifting his feet shamefacedly on the pavement. "She kept me on the boil all afternoon," he said. "I never even reached her knickers. What d'she expect was going to happen?"

"You must have reached something," I told him. "She wouldn't have belted you otherwise."

"Look on it as being rescued," he grinned. "You didn't have much hope there with Edith, now did you? The nearest you got to her was sitting by her in the pictures." He was almost smirking.

It was getting late, and home, even if it was in dry dock, was not far away up the road. By the number of our shipmates we met on the way back we were not the only ones with that idea.

The seamen's mess deck right forward was brightly lit, and seemed well filled with all our crew aboard. Men were getting out of their best suits, (number ones) and stowing them away in their lockers, others were slinging their hammocks ready to get turned in. Groups were sitting at the tables telling of their nights adventures, and a large pot of strong tea was being well used. Some of the duty watch who had not been ashore were already asleep, others in their hammocks were leaning over and taking part in the conversations that were going on.

It would take a while yet for the mess-deck to quieten down, but you got used to people walking about and talking below your hammock. Lights would dim as one after another lamps were turned off, and numbers around the table would dwindle as more and more turned in. Talk would become subdued, and often in whispers, until finally only the police lights would be left burning, and latecomers from shore leave would tip-toe in and undress in silence.

It would be the job of the Duty Petty Officer to wake everybody up in the morning, but this was hardly necessary. There would always be the early risers who would have the tea made. Besides, the banging of cups, the lashing and stowing of hammocks, the rushing off to get washed and shaved, and the dashing back to return toothbrushes, etc. to lockers, could be guaranteed to get all but the worst with hangovers ready on time. It was not unusual for heavy sleepers to be shaken awake, and have a cup of tea handed up to them.

Breakfast on the *Wellington* was just a polite term for a cup of tea, we seldom had time for such a luxury. There was bread and butter, and usually some jam around as well for those who felt they needed it. The *Wellington* had what was called canteen messing, in which a sum of money for each man in the mess was credited to the mess account. The Leading Seaman of that mess then had to buy the food for the mess from the NAAFI shop on board. No money changed hands, it was all done with chits of paper. Some provisions were supplied by the ship's store, such as fresh meat, tinned veg, milk, tea and sugar. Bread and spuds were also a daily issue.

Most times it balanced out, but if you wanted to live well you would have to pay for it with a whip round to settle a mess bill. Bacon and eggs for breakfast was regarded as living too well on a ship like the *Wellington.*

It was obvious to all of us that our life of ease was coming to an end. More and more workmen were swarming over our ship to get her ready by the due date.

During lunch break the following day, Fred and I clambered down the big steps at the side of the dock and walked underneath our ship. She had been scraped clean down to the bare metal and then freshly painted. She was sitting dead centre on huge wooden chocks that were as high as we were, and we were careful not to stand for long under any pipe openings just in case someone forgot about not flushing those toilet pans.

Right aft, her two gleaming propellers seemed to be bigger than we were. It was no wonder they could shake the whole ship whenever they had a reason to. The asdic dome, like some huge boot, was bolted to her bottom about on a level with A gun. We walked round it, kicking it fondly. I felt uneasy with all that bulk of metal bulging over me. Those wooden chocks suddenly seemed very vulnerable, and I almost ran out from underneath her. We climbed back up on the other side of the dock through a tunnel that had more normal steps than the side of the dock.

During the afternoon cables and stages were lifted out, and water began pouring in at both ends. Soon, water was rising over the chocks and lapping at her sides. The thick timber props that were holding her upright began coming loose, and we could feel her moving gently, as if she was glad to be free. Everything began coming alive. There was water on the taps again, the lights seemed brighter as her own generators took over. The ventilators began blasting out cold, fresh air, and arms were hastily raised to turn off the eyeball's. There was that low hum and gentle vibration of machinery, and pipes began hammering as steam rushed through.

Her upper decks were filthy and littered with dockyard tools, and until they had been cleared there wasn't much we could do about it. It had been nearly two months since water had been available on the hoses, so it was going to take us a long time to get those decks back to the snowy white state they were usually in. Two more depth charge throwers had been fitted on her quarterdeck, so she would be carrying a bigger punch than before. There would be eight charges to a pattern now, not five.

There was a new mast fitted on the quarterdeck, with something that looked like a bird cage on the top of it. We had also lost our three inch anti-aircraft gun from in front of the bridge. That had been lifted out by one of the big, dockside cranes. In its place was what looked like a bed of nails. It was about as big as a bed, and full of rows of spikes, all leaning slightly forward. We had heard about this new anti-submarine weapon called a Hedgehog.

Early next morning, two tugs took us in tow, and soon the *Wellington* was lined up facing some mud flats. They must have done that job before of course, as they seemed to know exactly where our pet Hedgehog would drop its young.

On each of the spikes we loaded a bomb shaped thing, and when they were all covered, they were fired by turning a wheel. There was a continuous roar as each of them fired in turn until they were all in the air together, and we all gasped as they dropped into the mud, making little splashes in a large perfect circle, with the last one plopping down right in the centre.

They had been blank bombs, to be recovered later. The real ones would have impact nose fuses. Satisfied that our Hedgehog was prickly enough, the tugs returned us to our berth, and soon, we had our ship back.

We might have lost our three-inch gun, but we had acquired many other far more dangerous one's. Gun platforms had been built wherever there was room for one to hold the new, Oerlikon anti-aircraft weapons that were spaced along her decks. A thick electrical cable had been fitted along her scuppers from stem to stern, when power was pushed through that, it was hoped that she could pass over magnetic mines without setting them off.

The lorries began arriving, and between loading stores and ammunition, the hoses were washing away some of the dirt of the land. Drums of hot water, with many pounds of soft soap added, were positioned along the upper deck, and with buckets of this hot, soapy mixture swilling over the grubby woodwork, lines of sailors using long handled scrubbing brushes, started from right forward at her breakwater, around both sides of the Captain's cabin, up onto B deck, which had now become the Hedgehog deck, each side of the wheelhouse, down the ladder, along the boat deck, then down on to the quarterdeck and both waists, among the depth charges, right to the stern. There was a marked difference in her filthy state even after this first scrubbing.

Starting at the Breakwater once more, with the salt water hoses turned on, scrubbing dirt and soap off, she was beginning to look more like our *Wellington* all the time.

Black smoke lifted from her funnel, and a heat haze shimmered above it. A thin trail of steam drifted away from her siren. Up in the wheelhouse, the green face of the giro was steadying after its erratic antics on first switch on. A small tanker had already been alongside, carefully fended off from our new paintwork, delivered her cargo, and left. Ammunition and stores were all aboard.

No shore leave had been piped for today, we had all been far too busy to allow that, so if Edith and Margery were hoping to meet us they would believe that we didn't care. But perhaps they would see us leaving, and would know that it wasn't our fault.

A cold wind was blowing, with a hint of rain. Much of the dirt of the land had been washed away, and HMS *Wellington* tugged at her mooring wires in Sheerness as if eager now to be away into the element that she was built for.

There was no tannoy system below decks, as she wasn't big enough for it to be necessary. At sea, it was the Bosun's Mate, a grand name for the wheelhouse dogsbody from the watch on deck, who would come round blowing a bosun's pipe and shouting a message.

In harbour, it was the Quartermaster, another good name for a gangway minder, who came round piping orders. If anyone wanted to know who was ashore, or anyone wanted to come aboard, you asked the Quartermaster. In most instances, he was armed with a loaded service revolver.

Supper over, and the dishes washed, and this time put safely away, the rain had set in with a vengeance. We could hear the Quartermaster shouting his message as he came forward. Those so familiar orders, piped before the start of every voyage.

"Close all watertight doors and scuttles. Special sea dutymen to your stations. Hands to positions for leaving harbour."

Oilskins were buttoned up, sou'westers tightened, towels tucked in around necks, a quick feel underneath, yes, Mae West was there, not blown up, that would have been too bulky: the rain feeling cold on your face as you gained the upper deck and already beginning to drip off your chin as you made your way along; The lapping of the water between the ship's side and the dock wall, as if they were chuckling together at some shared joke.

The shouts from the bridge. "Let go forrard." The shriek of the phone on the quarterdeck, and the shouted orders that followed it. "Let go aft. Hold on to your spring." The clang of the engine-room telegraphs, and the answering rush of water under her stern.

Held now only by that spring, her bows began coming out as she pulled astern. The thunder of water against the dock wall sounded as if friends were shouting goodbye. Then a moment of silence as her screws stopped churning.

"Let go springs." A rush of angry white foam lashed out at the dock wall as she thrust ahead. We could feel her bows lifting as she made for the sea. The rain beat harder against our oilskins as we reeled away the ropes and wires. Goodbye Sheerness, goodbye Edith and Marge, remember us sometimes.

Was that someone I could see near one of the shelters on the prom waving to us? It would be hardly likely on such a night, but just in case it was, I waved silently back.

A thorough check to make sure there were no lights showing as the safety of the land faded behind us. The towel around my neck was getting damp as it soaked up the rain running down my face. Soon now we would begin the familiar sea routine with lookouts to the bridge and quarters, and the watch on deck in the comparative shelter of the gun turrets. There might be some new faces among the crew after her long spell in harbour, but there were enough experienced one's to look after them, and they would learn fast. HMS *Wellington* was no new recruit joining the fray, but a seasoned campaigner returning from the safety of a refit to join her hard pressed comrades in the rapidly increasing danger zone of the Atlantic.

By the time we reached the approaches to Liverpool most of the dirt from Sheerness dockyard had been scrubbed away. You could say the same for her crew as well, most of them had been sick during the first night at sea as she made her way through the darkness of the English Channel. Up through the southern Irish Sea towards the approaches to Liverpool, and before she entered the swept channel her new de-gausing cables were energised to protect her against any of those magnetic mines that had been causing so much trouble to unprotected ships.

There were not many warships left inside Gladstone dock, and we couldn't help but notice the mass of ships assembling outside in the river. As we tied up alongside the wall, our new Oerlikon anti-aircraft guns, and the Hedgehog excited attention from crew members of other ships, and many came aboard to see them at close hand.

There was mail waiting for us, and there was a letter for me from Lorna. There was no address on it, but it did have a Southport stamp. She was to marry a train driver in a few months' time, and they intended going to Plymouth for their honeymoon.

Plymouth! How dare she. How could she walk with her husband over the grass of Plymouth Hoe after what we had been doing on it? Would she say, "Oh, look darling, this grass is still crushed where I was lying on it." Why couldn't she take him to Blackpool, or somewhere. And a train driver as well. Spitefully, I thought he would have to be a lot older than she was if he was a train driver.

After a few minutes of anger, it didn't seem to matter. To our surprise, all night leave was piped, but it was obvious to all of us that this would be the last time ashore for some while.

Fred looked at me, and without a word being spoken we changed into our number ones, fished out the silk stockings and scents we had bought in Gibraltar, and fell in on the quarterdeck for inspection as Libertymen. Then we were off to Southport.

The ladies in the cafe near the station greeted us like lost brothers, and when we presented our gifts they produced food from the back room of that cafe that reminded us of blessed peace time. We kept some of our gifts for Mrs Jones at our boarding house, and she made us welcome and gave us the same room before she saw what we had brought her.

Later that afternoon we called at the hospital, and I waited outside as Fred went in to ask about Kitty. He wasn't in there long, and came out walking slowly with his hands in his pocket.

I watched him silently as we both stood on the pavement, waiting for him to speak.

"They knew her," he said after a while. "She died nearly two months ago." He still had his hands in his pockets.

I remembered her cold hands, and those dark shadows under her big eyes.

"What should I do with this?" he asked me, as he held out his hand. A little silver cross dangled from a tiny chain. I thought for a moment that he was going to hurl it away, but it was a nearby tin he kicked, and it went way down the road under the force of the blow. He put the cross and chain back in his pocket and walked off, and I hurried after him.

That evening, we met Dot and Alice, and the future for both of us began to look bright again. To heck with Lorna. If the weather was warmer Alice would look just as nice in a bathing suit as she had. We had a great evening, and got them back to the railway station just in time for them to catch their train. We didn't dare make a date to meet them again, as we knew we wouldn't be able to keep it. But we had their address, we would write.

The smoke hung over Liverpool as we walked back from the station early next morning. Out in the river many ships were moving as one convoy prepared to leave just as another was coming in. As the escorts came into the lock from the river and waited for the dock gates to open, we eyed them keenly, looking for signs of damage, noting the toll of the weather. One after the other, they tied up in different parts of the dock, and almost as soon as they were safely inside, we began moving out.

The escorts were now operating in groups of five, and HMS *Wellington* was leader of Group 52. The five ships would work together, exercise together, fight together. They would become a close knit band, highly experienced, and highly dangerous against the quarry they were built for.

Submarines were also working in groups, and once a convoy had been spotted it called up others in the area to the kill. Our new birdcage atop its mast would pick up that radio call, and point to where it came from.

It was an eerie feeling, as darkness lowered over the sea, to hear those submarines reporting as they closed in on their intended victims. We would go early to action stations on the Pipe, not on the alarm bells. Doors and hatches would close, ammunition ready use lockers open, fire and cease fire bells checked, anti flash gloves and helmets in your pockets, Mae West lifebelts on and blown up this time.

Silence would descend over the whole ship. The whine of the turbines and the throbbing of the screws wouldn't drown the pinging of the asdic as the unseen beam probed for the approaching danger. Often, the first warning would be a brilliant white flash from somewhere in the convoy, followed by the heavy thump of the explosion. Sometimes the asdic would hear the torpedo running. And sometimes it would be the double ping as contact was made.

One thing was for certain. There wasn't a man on any of those warships who wouldn't take his hat off to the crews of those merchant ships. They were the target every time.

When a submarine pack did strike, it could be a massacre. Ship after ship would be sunk, and the track of the convoy littered with lifeboats and wreckage. We never left survivors behind for long, one or other of the escorts would be detached next morning to go get them.

One morning we picked up two boat loads of Indian seamen and transferred them later in the day to another ship in the convoy. That night, more ships were torpedoed, and next morning saw us hauling the very same Indians back on board the *Wellington* again. This time they refused to be sent to another ship, so we offered them accommodation in the tiller flat, a space back aft where the steering engine lived and shuddered. In no time at all they had it scrubbed out, polished, and carpeted with survivors blankets. All the heaving lines, ropes, and blocks that we had thrown in there were all neatly hanging along the bulkheads, and even our Chief Engineer seemed delighted with the way his steering engine stopped shaking the ship.

Each evening, just before dark, the *Wellington* would cruise up and down between the lines of ships looking for any lights that had been left on. We had left one ship behind, and was coming up fast on another, passing her wake, when she suddenly exploded. From being a lovely ship, with thirty or more people living and laughing, it was instant death as she turned into a rising pillar of heat and flame, going up and up with fiery flares and smaller explosions shooting sideways out of it. To everyone on the upper deck it felt like being smacked in the face with a hot, wet, towel.

There were splashes over a wide area of sea where pieces of ship and cargo began dropping back, and in less than thirty seconds there was just a greasy patch on the restless ocean, and a gap in the line where once a ship had been. There could be no survivors from such an end, but we would cross and re-cross that greasy patch, hoping against hope that we would see something moving in the water, but we never did.

As we progressed southwards the weather got warmer and more pleasant. Duffle coats and balaclava's would give way to white shirts and shorts. The crew would settle into a routine of scrubbing and cleaning, painting and oiling.

Chapter Seven

Saturday morning was always Captain's rounds day, when mess-decks would be spotless, tables and forms scrubbed white, cutlery polished and laid out in fan shaped designs. Kettles, fannies and all pots were burnished and displayed on the mess deck table for the inspection. Any article of clothing or belongings that was not put away in the owner's locker was gathered up in a big sack called the scranbag, to be recovered later at the cost of a bar of soap. Everyone was far too busy on a Saturday morning to worry about preparing dinner. Besides, the galley would come in for inspection as well during Captain's rounds, so our cooks would not want to spend much time cooking. Saturday dinner was corned beef day, with whatever tinned veg we dared open.

Every mess had its Gash Running Party, Gash being a name given to anything that was spare. If there wasn't time to clean something, or if anything was left over that just couldn't be put away, the Gash Running Party would be carrying it down one passage as the Captain and his Inspecting Officers walked up the other. If all else failed, half a potato would be left on the table in full view. This would usually cause so much consternation and discussion amongst the Inspecting Party that they would fail to notice anything else amiss.

Saturday morning was devoted to scrubbing decks. Lines of

sailors, wearing seaboots in cold weather or barefoot if it was warm, scrubbed from forward to aft with hot, soapy water, and then washed down with salt water hoses. The wooden decks came up sparkling white. At eleven o'clock, as on every other morning, UP SPIRITS was piped by the Bosun's Mate. This was the signal for the Leading Seamen of the messes to attend outside the galley. Here, under the eagle eyes of the Duty Officer, Duty P.O. and the Jaunty, tots were dispensed from a brass-bound oak barrel bearing the words THE KING, GOD BLESS HIM.

The Chief's and Petty Officers had their ration as neat spirit, other ranks would have water added before it was filled into their fannies. These fannies would then be borne back to their respective messes, and the Leading Seaman would dish out a measure to those entitled as they arrived. Any favours or birthdays would be paid for as sippers right there at the end of the table. There was no time to languish about and enjoy a drink as you would in a pub, you were expected to gulp it down in one go and hand back the cup ready for the next man. The final act of the ritual would be the tipping away of any spirit left over in the barrel down that spotless galley sink, watched despairingly and helplessly by all the members of the party. They didn't have to go into the galley to do that, it was always done through an open window from the passage, watched by our Petty Officer Chef, who never failed to find something to do at his range during this time.

On Sunday morning at sea there was always church. The crew would dress in number ones, and the Bosun's Mate would come round piping "Clear lower deck. Hands to church on the quarterdeck." If the weather wasn't suitable, then it would be held on the Stoker's mess deck. Our Captain would read verses from the Bible, and we would all join in the Lords Prayer.

In fine, warm weather the evenings could be quite pleasant. Off duty men would stroll around our very limited deck space, in spotless whites. The galley hatches would be open and the smell of cooking helping to work up an appetite.

Dolphins! The cry would go up, and people would crowd to the rails to watch them as they converged on the ship, easily outpacing us at our fastest speed. They would leap around our bows, evidently enjoying themselves, and would stay with us for about fifteen minutes, then vanish just as quickly as they had come.

Ludo, was a game we often played on the upper deck in warm weather. Someone would unroll a canvas sheet as big as three blankets, the dice was as big as a kilo of sugar, and it was shook in a bucket. The shouts that went up could be heard on ships in the convoy.

We liked nothing better at this time than to steam between the lines of ships of the convoy at evening time checking on lighted portholes, waving to crews on the other ships passing so close. Sometimes there were women aboard them, and we would stare in disbelief to see them sharing such danger as their menfolk. If there was more than one, or a group of them, they would be daring, and lift their clothes, sometimes even showing their knickers. Half the crew of HMS *Wellington* would be in danger of falling overboard at such a moment.

Travelling fast at 270 revolutions with a white wake creaming far behind her, the *Wellington* was quickly regaining station when a corvette out on the right began blasting on her siren. We looked at each other, counting. "Four, five, six. Submarine to starboard!"

Racing to action stations even before the alarm bells, we could see them. Torpedoes! Fired from extreme range, they were now travelling on the surface. Six of them. Leaping like dolphins only much bigger, coming flashing along in a fan shaped salvoe. One passed within ten feet of our bows, and another went through the white wake.

All of our Port Oerlikon anti-aircraft guns opened fire on them as they passed to that side, which was a measure of how quickly the watch on deck brought them into action. There was a horrific explosion as we hit one of them, then the splashes were in amongst the ships of the convoy, and we held our breath as we watched.

Miraculously, none of them were hit. It was also a lesson to all of us who were on the upper deck at that time. None of us had our lifebelts with us, and two torpedoes had missed us quite literally by just feet.

Travelling at full speed now, we joined with the corvette in a hunt that lasted all night long, and ended next forenoon with our spotless whites of last night now grubby and blackened with smoke.

As our convoy dispersed at Gibraltar the *Wellington* entered harbour with her crew lined up along the forecastle and quarterdeck. There was a massive British Naval force in the harbour, and we whistled silently as we saw them. The pubs in Main Street would be full tonight. From the signal tower a light was blinking at us, and we altered course from the mole towards the oiler.

To be quite honest, there wasn't much room anywhere for us to berth, the place seemed to be overflowing with warships. We thought hopefully that some of them might have the honour of taking the next convoy home while we got in some sun bathing.

From the oiler we were directed to drop anchor in the Bay, and a trot boat brought us our mail. I had a letter from Alice, with a card inside for Fred from Dot. She hoped that we were enjoying ourselves wherever we were. Reminded us that we had promised to write, and they were going to a dance next week, and we could take them if they heard from us in time.

Not much chance of that, we agreed. Here we were, stuck at sea in the shadow of Gibraltar, too far out even to smell Ivy Benson's perfume. There was an unusual motion about the *Wellington* as well. She was not used to being at anchor, or her cable was a bit short. It kept jerking her and throwing us off balance.

When the Bosun's Mate piped shore leave from 1900 to 2300 it was better than nothing. Too late for the theatre, and the shops would be shut, so the silk undies we had been thinking of would have to wait. What would Alice look like in some of the things we had seen hanging in the shops along Main Street? Perhaps, if they were sheer enough she would . . .

"You're dribbling!" accused Fred, staring.

I grinned at him. "No I'm not. Just hoping."

I grimaced as the trot boat came alongside our gangway, and could feel the paint being scraped off as though it was skin. Everyone glared at the Leading Seaman Coxswain, as we would have to put that paint back on again.

We watched the lights of the *Wellington* fading away behind us, it was such a novelty to see lights at all that it took a bit of getting used to. Other boats were crossing about in the harbour, there was a lot of traffic between the many ships and the jetties.

Some of the shops were open, and just in case we might not have another chance we bought what we thought we could use. I laughed out loud as I watched Fred modelling a pair of silk knickers he hopefully intended to put on Dot. Only later did I realise that the shopkeeper was looking at me very suspiciously and keeping well behind his counter.

Some of our gang were there in Ivy's, and they made room at the table for us. The place was packed, the waiters were having to push through with the drinks. The tables were soon full of glasses, roast chickens were going the rounds, and the prawns and shrimps were being sampled, salt and vinegar being sprinkled and splashed. Singing often drowned out the sound of the band. Arguments would develop, voices raised. Patrols would make a salutary appearance, just walking in and straight out again, and I asked Fred if he thought his silk knickers would fit; they had looked a bit big to me when he held them in front of him at the shop.

There was a moment of silence as the rest of the table digested this, then eager hands helped him remove his trousers. In deference to Ivy's group, who couldn't see what was going on anyway, they let him keep his underpants on. We put the knicker's on him, his trousers were solemnly packed up in the parcel, placed under his arm, he was pointed at the doorway, and off he went.

We were all thrown out a few minutes later in time to be back aboard our different ships. Miraculously, Fred and his knickers were waiting safely on the jetty. He had walked through Main Street undetected by any of the patrols.

We would often take passengers with us from Gibraltar on our convoy voyages back to the United Kingdom. They usually had quarters back aft with our Officers, but it must have been a long and boring journey for them with nothing to do, and very little space for them to do it in.

We shamelessly made use of them by having them give talks to the off duty crew. One of the RAF Officers taking passage told us about the problems of training new pilots from abroad, using the phrase 'old whores pretending to be virgins'. "I came to Gib in a Sunderland flying boat in six hours", he told us, "and I'm going back on the *Wellington* taking three weeks".

Another man who took passage with us was Jarche, a photographer for *Picture Post.* He took that wonderful picture of the guns of London firing at night during one of the air raids. He took many pictures of HMS *Wellington* while she was at sea during the voyage. I still have the centre spread of *Illustrated,* dated February 15th, 1941. We were at church that Sunday morning on the quarterdeck, and he took the picture from alongside B gun, with the ship's company in whites, and the convoy safely astern of us.

If he had any memories of the *Wellington,* it would have to be of the night we all thought she had been torpedoed. The weather had worsened as we proceeded northwards, and a cold, drizzly rain had set in by evening time.

As the visibility decreased, the escorts closed in on their convoy, and the wind and sea got more severe as the darkness added to our problems. Unable to increase speed for fear of losing the convoy we had to endure a following sea that time after time swept up on us out of the darkness and smashed down on the low quarterdeck.

The Quartermaster's on the wheel had an impossible task trying to keep her on course as many tons of white water toppled out of the night onto her stern. The watertight doors on each side had long since been shut tight to keep the sea out of the passages, and the ladder from the boat deck down to the quarterdeck had been roped off to prevent any unthinking sailor from trying to walk on the open deck.

Just after midnight, when the watch on deck had changed, one of those accidents that seemed impossible happened. An overtaking sea, sweeping up from behind, raced over the low deck, frothing among the depth charges, and somehow managed to lift a depth charge, lashed to a carrier, up and out of the stand where they stood ready to be hoisted into the thrower. There were four of these charges round each of the throwers, waiting ready to be loaded after the one always kept ready for firing in the thrower had gone. They were so heavy, it took a derrick and tackle to lift one, or, so it seemed, a high following sea.

Unknown to anyone, this depth charge, still lashed to a carrier, was sinking slowly beneath us.

On each charge there was a clock with a brass key for setting the depth at which it would explode, and the key could not be removed until a depth had been set on it. If twenty charges had been fired during an attack, then twenty keys had to be produced to show they had been lethal. There was also a primer held safely away by a compressed rubber washer from the depth clock with its dangerous detonator. All of these precautions should have ensured our safety, but what was about to happen showed all on board what he could expect if the worst should ever occur.

The increasing water pressure on the primer forced it up against the detonator in the depth clock with such force that good British workmanship ensured that it did its work. The force of the explosion lifted the whole ship, but miraculously there was no damage above deck other than an unexpected funnel cleaning, and the galley chimneys emptied all their load of soot over everything nearby.

One of the first on deck was Jarche, in pyjamas, mark you, garments we hadn't seen since Civvy Street. It all brought back memories of the Duchess as hurrying sailors, checking for damage, stopped running, walked round him staring, then hurried off again.

Below decks there was chaos. Dishes had jumped out of lockers, tea, sugar, and flour had scattered everywhere, light bulbs were smashed. From one of the escorts a dim light asked anxiously if we had been torpedoed, and later, from the Commodore, came "Aye, aye, what's all this then?"

One passenger was given accommodation in the sick bay. We never saw him, except through the door left accidently open when we were passing. He was older than we were, had grey hair, and was always dressed in overalls. One night I was sitting on a stool in the wheelhouse doing my turn at the wheel. The Petty Officer of the Watch was away on his rounds, and the Bosun's Mate had gone down to get us a cup of cocoa. I could hear the Officer of the Watch on the bridge above talking to the Signalman, and then there were footsteps coming up the ladder from below which I assumed was the cocoa coming.

At the end of a zig-zag I got the expected order to change course and I stood up to answer, and bumped into someone standing behind me. It was our passenger from the sick bay, and he was holding a carving knife that he had collected from the Stokers mess on the way up. He began talking to someone above his left shoulder, happily enough at first, laughing at the replies he seemed to be receiving, then he began to get angry, and started lashing out with the knife at whatever it was he was talking to.

The ship was already beginning to answer her helm and come around, so I couldn't just make a fast exit or she would soon be heading back at the convoy, but the carving knife was flashing about dangerously near the back of my neck. Subby, the Bosun's

Mate, came clattering up the ladder holding two mugs of steaming cocoa in one hand, saw what was happening, and promptly went back down again.

Pressed hard against the wheel to avoid the carving knife, I slipped sideways towards the revolution counter and turned to face the passenger, easing the wheel from there to stop her turning too far off course. He made no move to come after me, his quarrel was with whoever it was behind his right shoulder.

Footsteps, more than one pair this time, came clambering up from below, and first into view came Doc, eyes wide and staring behind his big glasses. Without hesitation he clapped our passenger on the shoulder.

"Come on, Jim," he said calmly, "let's go down. Gimme that." And he snatched the knife out of the passenger's hand. Together, they went down the ladder.

I glared at Subby. "Why in hell didn't you throw the cocoa over him. You saw what he was doing. He could have cut my bloody head off!"

Subby was unconcerned, a dewdrop formed on his nose. "You would have looked much better that way," he grinned, "and why waste good cocoa? I got Doc to save you, didn't I?"

I couldn't argue with that part of it. At least the cocoa was hot, but unsweetened. It seemed we were out of sugar again.

The snow covered hills of Scotland was our first indication of the severe weather the U.K. was suffering from: As we shivered under our duffle coats, balaclavas, mittens, and seaboot socks, we thought that now we could understand why no one in Gib seemed eager to take our convoy home.

Line after line of heavily laden merchant ships wallowed in our wake as we made for the Clyde. We would be safely in the river before nightfall, and with any luck would get the first decent night's sleep for three weeks. For once, it was safe to disregard the smoke pouring from dozens of ship's funnels as they cracked on speed anticipating a safe night in harbour after the weeks of strain they had come through. We slowed and pulled aside to let them pass as they made eagerly for the channel.

Each of them blasted away on their whistle as they went by, and all on deck waved. What remained of wind torn ensigns fluttered proudly at their sterns. Some remembered their manners and hurriedly dipped them as they passed, others saw them do it and wondered why, and we grinned as they blissfully ignored us as they jostled for position in line ahead up the river. Some were so big they seemed to take ages to pass, and we were so near we were looking up at their crew as they waved. A seemingly endless line of ships, all full of vitally needed cargoes, snaked their way towards their different berths.

The escorts made up the last of the line, and we made for the oiler anchored in the river that was waiting to receive us. The G.P.O. had done its stuff once more: there were the sacks of mail on the deck ready for us to collect.

There were lots of wild rumours circulating as usual, but one seemed stronger than normal. Our home base was to be shifted further northwards, Greenock seemed to be the favourite, so it looked like we had seen the last of our friendly Liverpool.

I recognised Alice's handwriting on the envelope of one of my letters. I read about the dance she had been to. She and Dot had been there, but it hadn't been much fun without us. They were both looking forward to hearing from us, please write whenever we could.

Ruefully I folded her letter back into the envelope. Liverpool and Southport seemed another world away. I looked along the table to where Fred was reading his mail. He seemed to be getting more of it than me, but I waved the envelope until I caught his eye, "From Alice."

He held up the sheet he was reading, "From Dot."

We looked at each other sympathetically, and went back to reading our mail. There was one there from Sue, I recognised her writing as I held the envelope. I remembered how she had looked back at me from the ward door at the hospital in Portsmouth, the fights we had at school, the way she pulled my hair when she couldn't get her own way, and the tree she couldn't climb to get at me after I had thumped her when she wasn't looking.

I should have told her there at the hospital how lovely she had become, and promised to climb a much lower tree if I ever hit her again. I should have told her then I intended to marry her one day, but I had been too shy. It was not a gauche schoolgirl I would have been talking to, but a beautiful girl, while I had been just a sick and thin sailor. She would probably have laughed in my face.

Before I could open her letter the Bosun's Mate was piping for hands to stand by wires and fenders. We moved away from the oiler to make way for other escorts, and further up river came gently alongside one of the bigger ships that had been part of our convoy.

Her crew welcomed us as if we were old friends, and gladly helped with our wires and ropes. As we were going to be there for the night, we rigged a gangway between the two ships, but we were smaller than they were, and moved up and down with the swell, so using the gangway was like walking the plank. While no one fell overboard, several came near it. After supper, leaning on the guard-rails with cups, jars, or whatever was available, of tea in our hands, chatting to the crew of the merchantman, it emerged that our tea was unsweetened because of the usual shortage of sugar.

This seemed to cause consternation among our new friends. There was a hurried discussion, then suddenly their deck winches started clanking, wedges removed, hatchcovers opened, and we found ourselves looking down through a small opening at a space that looked the size of an aircraft hangar full of big, brown sacks. Some of her crew climbed down with strops, and soon the winches were lifting bundles of these sacks out of the hold and swinging them across to our deck.

We couldn't believe our eyes. Gorgeous, gleaming, brown sugar.

Tons of it. Like liquid gold cascading from burst sacks into our scuppers. In no time at all there was a huge pile of sacks that threatened to give us a list. We had to shout, "Whoa! What are we going to do with it all?" Each mess took a sack, and struggled off with it, then had the problem of trying to store it among pots and biscuit tins.

HMS *Wellington* was due a boiler clean. It was fortunate for the crews that their ships had to be pulled out for repairs and maintenance now and again. We knew roughly when these intervals were, but if things were going badly, or if a convoy was under attack, then repairs or boiler cleaning would just have to wait.

There was a post box outside the Jaunty's office, and all mail from HM ships was posted free. In harbour, the box would be emptied every day, letters would be censored, and sent on their way. It was pointless posting letters while we were at sea, and the box would be sealed. But if there was a chance of sending letters home, say, from a passing destroyer, or by extra escorts which were now turning back after helping a convoy through a particular dangerous area, then there would be a pipe throughout the ship. Mail will close at 1500, or whatever, and later, at the appropriate time, the two ships would converge and steam along close to each other without stopping, passing a bag of mail across by Coston gun line. There would be waves, and hoots on the sirens, and both ships would turn away. We would write letters at sea, that was one of the main occupations, but we couldn't post them.

Sipping unaccustomed sweet tea, I took Sue's letter from my locker and wondered if the coal miner I had last seen her with . . . What was his name? Tom, was it? Had I lost her to someone more forceful than I had proved to be? I opened the envelope and took out a single page letter.

She hoped I was fit and well by now, and she was back at work in Croydon. Next time I should visit Chatham she would expect me to make the effort to reach her as she had done to reach me.

All at home were well, and write to your mother as often as you possibly can as she looks forward so much to your letters. She worries so much when they become overdue. Take care, and perhaps we will meet next time you are home. That was all. I looked on the other side of the page, but there was no more. There was no mention of Tom.

I well knew how my mother used to watch for my letters. It was a crucifying time for all the mothers in the world. We had a kind of code involving girl's names. She was always curious about the girls I had met, and never believed my description of some beautiful creature who I had met in a church just after she had left a convent, but the names she believed. So when I said in my censored letter that I saw Lorna yesterday, she would understand that I was in Plymouth. If I said I had taken Alice to a show last night, that would be Liverpool, if I talked about Madge, she would guess Glasgow.

Thinking about Madge it looked like we would be staying here in the Clyde for a boiler clean, if we wrote now the mail would be off the ship this evening and could be delivered by tomorrow. There would be shore leave tomorrow, and we could meet Ruth and Madge in Glasgow.

Further along the table that was Two mess, Fred was already writing. Although it was only early evening, tied up securely alongside our big neighbour, safely home in the Clyde, one after the other, men slung their hammocks, and by eight o'clock, only the police lights were left burning. Except for a Signalman and the Quartermaster, the ship's company of HMS *Wellington* was fast asleep.

Early next morning, with the smoke from the chimney's along the waterfront barely visible in the cold, dawn light, we left the safety of our big freighter and headed down river with bitter thoughts and increasing speed. An outward bound convoy for Halifax was under attack from submarines and aircraft. HMS *Wellington* would rendezvous with two destroyers coming from Devonport to give support.

Smashing her way up through the North Channel, snorting icy water back over A gun turret, we huddled in the lee of the bridge superstructure, feeling the warmth from the galley hatches. Soon, outside the railway station in Glasgow, Ruth and Madge would arrive, expecting to see us there waiting for them, as Fred had promised.

'Please, Madge. It's not our fault.' But it would be asking a lot to expect them to understand. Especially after getting his letter that morning telling them we would be there. Our mail had gone off last night by trot boat, so they would have had the letter.

Two days later, after risking damage at full speed from a strong head wind, smudges of smoke on the horizon showed up the convoy. But wreckage we had passed long before that showed how desperately they needed any help that we could give. From off to the left the two destroyers, just shadows in the dusk, were also closing.

Even from that distance it was possible to see the leading destroyer hoisting the attack flag, and both ships slewed around like dogs sensing a fox, and at that moment the *Wellington* made asdic contact with something in the water ahead. The large, black attack flag fluttered aloft just in time for the destroyers to see it before the darkness closed in.

Whatever forces were trailing that convoy and jockeying for position for a night attack were in for a rude shock. We could already feel and hear the depth charges from the destroyers out there on our left, and the thing we were tracking seemed to be turning away as if puzzled by what was coming up behind him.

Ten seconds later he could have had no doubt what was on his trail. Sixteen depth charges went down in two attacks, but by midnight we had lost him. However we could still feel the shocks from the charges being dropped by the destroyers.

Ranging at full speed along the track of the convoy, sniffing at various contacts, sometimes dropping a full pattern on any likely echo, if there were submarines trailing that convoy they must have suffered some damage from all that high explosives sprinkled among them, and they would have had to remain stopped and silent while those warships hunted for them.

At dawn a Sunderland joined us, so we could crack on speed after the convoy now out of sight ahead, they wouldn't dare surface as long as that aircraft was there.

The convoy had suffered no further casualties during the night, and we liked to think that was due to our timely arrival interfering with a planned attack. But the convoy had been found, and its position no doubt reported. It was reasonable to expect that the enemy was directing everything he could lay hands on to intercept this Halifax bound mass of shipping.

Tired, cold and hungry, with damp clothes, we huddled at our gun positions as daylight spread over a grey sea. Mae Wests blown up, anti-flash gear on, watching grimly for the air attack that was sure to be planned. They would be coming for us, we knew, and would have taken off during the hours of darkness. The minutes ticked away as the light grew stronger. Gun barrels swung silently like questing fingers as their crews flexed their muscles and, like well trained sheepdogs, the warships closed up on their flock, huddling together as if to gain courage from the nearness of others.

I pushed my face into the rubber mask of the Oerlikon to hide the twitching of my dry mouth. The rings of the gun sight was clear now in the strengthening light. Something cold and unexpected touched my frightened face, and I pulled away from the mask to see what it was. Swinging on the gun sight was a little silver cross and chain.

I glanced at Fred standing white faced besides me, waiting to reload, our eyes met, and we both felt stronger for that help from Kitty. It would hang there every time we felt we needed it from now on.

At first we thought it was the noise of our own machinery, then the warning hoots from distant siren's before the gunnery orders over the headphones from fire control.

"Train left. Target red three five. All guns. Stand by. "The voice was calm, like a bored teacher talking to his class.

And there they were. Four black dots, low on the water, coming in fast. Within seconds it was possible to see they were four engine bombers, and they fanned out as they approached. They were so low the wind of their propellers caused a wake in the sea they were passing over.

The *Wellington* heaved as her 4.7s flung their shells at the nearest oncoming aircraft. Black bursts right in her path caused her to wheel, and the next salvoe seemed to be right underneath her. The fire bells for the Oerlikons brought a shuddering roar from the batteries amidships, and from the others near the wheelhouse as they pumped impact shells by the hundred. The fourth shell coming from each Oerlikon was a tracer, it burnt red as it flashed through the air, so it looked like HMS *Wellington* was fighting a fire using red water from a line of hosepipes along the ship.

There was fluttering flame coming from the gun positions on the aircraft as they came in, then they banked so as to fly along the line of ships, and the bombs began to drop. Each ship seemed to wait until the last moment as the aircraft ran up the wake, then they would try to turn aside to present only their width as a target instead of their length. Each of them had a gun of some sort, and was using it, one Captain we saw was using a rifle from his wheelhouse window.

Huge spouts of water were rising from amongst the lines of ships, and the sky above was black with shell bursts. At times we could not fire for fear of hitting other ships, and there were moments when we were in more danger than the attacking aircraft as enthusiastic gunners on our charges sent their shells screaming past our startled ears. Then it was all over as quickly as it had come.

The Halifax convoy was still intact, they hadn't hit one of them. We hoped the Sunderland way back there behind us had not been seen by the Focke-Wulfs that had attacked us, as it would have been no match for them.

The decks of the *Wellington* seemed to be knee deep in brass cartridge cases, and we ruefully looked at the burnt and blackened gun barrels of the 4.7s.

One of the watertight hatches opened, and there were cusses as someone pushed aside some blocking cartridge cases, then the welcome face of Chopper, from the ammunition supply, who was our boot repairer and hair cutter, looked up at us, and passed out a fanny of steaming tea, a handful of cups, and a pile of corned beef sandwiches.

Six days later, secured alongside the quay at Greenock, Fred passed over a letter from Ruth. She wasn't going to wait any more for him. She and her friend Madge had found two much more dependable boyfriends who were in the Army. They wouldn't keep her waiting at cold railway stations as we seem to like doing.

I thought she was quite right. In any case, I hadn't written, it was Fred who wrote and made the date. He seemed quite upset about this, and was already writing to make amends.

There was no doubt we would be in harbour for some time. Half the ship's company had gone home on ten days leave; it would be our turn next time, and dockyard maties were already dismantling the boiler room.The ship was very quiet with only half her crew aboard, and with half of them allowed all night shore leave it was an evening for reading and writing and early to bed.

Next day, with all night shore leave, we were off to Glasgow, and at seven o'clock were waiting hopefully for our girl friends outside the railway station, albeit, eight days late.

We saw them approaching and looked at each other uncomfortably as we saw they were on the arm of two Swaddies. I grinned at Madge as she went by and noted her wink. Fred was on the verge of going to battle stations and I thought it best to hold on to his arm as they disappeared into the station.

I wondered what would happen if we attacked, and here, I must admit, I was optimistic, as I was definitely bigger than any of those soldiers, a physical miscalculation on my mother's part I fear, as it meant that I was in great demand whenever patrols were required. We followed them into the station, only to see both army men escaping our wrath by getting on a train.

I grinned again as I watched Ruth cling to her soldier's neck as the train began to move, while Madge just stood back and waved. Just as it looked that poor Ruth would be swept off to the next station she let go just in time to avoid running off the platform, while Fred kicked the daylight's out of a nearby chocolate machine.

Madge came back to me, put her arms round my neck and kissed me in a way that made the porters whistle appreciatively, caused Fred to stop kicking the chocolate machine and made me forget where I was.

She pushed my hands away and tugged me towards the station gates. I followed in a dream, seeing Fred's open mouth stare as we went.

Recovering only slowly, I held her tight as we walked, hoping for more. "Who was that on the train?" I asked, nodding behind us. "It upset Fred."

"Didn't it upset you?" She turned her head to look at me. Her face was so close that I stopped walking. There was no other thought in my head except the memory of that embrace in the station. My arms went round her, and as I held her to me a low whistle from the passer's by brought me back to my senses. I was tingling all over in such a way that it was painful to walk. All night leave! Was this what the Navy had been saving me for?

There was an opening in the bushes alongside us and holding

her hand, I led her into the darkness. A welcoming tree seemed to hold out it's branches to caress us, and as I opened her coat and lifted her dress, she kissed me again as she had done in the station.

And Fred shouted, "Is that you in there?" He came blundering in, leaving Ruth standing on the pavement.

It was my turn to do the kicking bit, and I punished that tree, wishing with every kick that it was Fred's backside. As blithely innocent as I believed my sister to be, he was already out on the pavement with the girls.

In the Empire that night we saw Sandy Powell on the stage as a quick change artist, and roared with laughter as his helpers slung him through the different windows. And I clung tightly to Madge as a tramp wandered across the stage to rummage in a dustbin and found a violin; then played it so beautifully that it brought tears to every eye.

Back at the railway station, hungry, but unable to find anywhere to eat now at this time of night, Madge asked me to take her home. Fred and I could have found food with no problem at the Salvation Army Hostel or the YMCA, but we couldn't take our girls there, even if they had wanted to come.

I avoided Fred's enquiring stare. Up to now, our girls had taken us home, which was to the nearest bus or tram stop in order to prevent our Jaunty charging us with being absent without leave. But the Navy said we were men now; we could stay out all night if we wanted to.

I had no idea where I would spend tonight; some park bench probably. But Madge had asked me to take her home and that is what I would do. Fred could do whatever he felt like; I'd see him back aboard ship tomorrow. Without a backward glance we caught a tram towards some place called Knightsbridge, and left Fred and Ruth staring after us.

I took her all the way to the front door of a house at the end of a long street and in the darkness of the doorway I kissed her goodnight. She kissed me in the same way she had at the railway station, as I gasped for breath she opened the door behind her and drew me into the passage.

"That was my brother at the station," she whispered in my ear. "Tonight, this house is mine."

Feeling as breathless as I had under the tree, I held tightly to her hand as she took me to her room. I knew it was her room as soon as she opened the door; I could smell her perfume. We undressed in the dark alongside her single bed; then her warm body against mine drove all thoughts of Fred or food from my mind. Truly, the Navy would have to class me as a man from now on.

I awoke very early next morning by falling out of bed and thinking I had fallen out of my hammock, but I recovered quickly when I heard her peels of laughter. It was just as well that I had awoken early, as I had a long way to go to get back on board a ship at Greenock. But there was other things to do first, so I quickly got back under the warm clothes.

It was still dark as I slipped away down that long street, trying to remember the directions she had given me. I walked up the gangway of the *Wellington* with just minutes to spare, and studiously avoided Fred's stare while complaining bitterly about the hardness of Scottish park benches when forced to spend the night on one.

That seemed to satisfy everyone, even Fred.

Privileged envelopes, a distinctive green colour, issued just one a month at first, was a great idea. Using one, it meant that mail would not be censored on the ship but we were warned that it could still be censored by departments ashore. Any number of letters could be inserted into that one envelope, but that would mean the recipient would have to stamp them and send them on to whoever they were addressed to. Usually, it was only the one letter these envelopes contained, as there wasn't much you were ashamed of in those days of your youth; only the older men resented local censorship. During that boiler clean, while over the side on a stage touching up the paintwork of our camouflage, Fred emptied a whole gallon of grey paint into the river beneath him because he thought it was the wrong colour.

The Petty Officer who had mixed it in the paint store was incensed, as anybody would have been in his place, and there was no excuse for Fred, as a bit of black would have darkened it or a dash of white would have lightened it.

He was taken before the Duty Officer and the only punishment possible was the First Lieutenants report.

Next morning, with the Duty Petty Officer present and the Duty Officer, and all of them properly dressed in the rig of the day, the Jaunty ordered "Off cap," and read out the charge to the First Lieutenant.

The punishment was five days leave stopped, which he deserved, but that meant I had two girls on my arm in Glasgow the following night, and I claim that was more punishment than he had, as then I couldn't do anything to either of them. I put them both on a tram after kissing Ruth on the forehead with a mumbled, "Bless you by, sister," while hoping she wouldn't feel anything resting against her leg.

Unknown to any of us, our stupid Fred was pouring his heart out in a letter to Ruth. What he called our Officers for daring to stop his leave was nobody's business. All of this went into a privileged envelope and was posted aboard, and by sheer bad luck, was caught in the censorship net ashore and sent back to the ship.

It was the Captain's report this time and he judged it serious enough to have Fred transferred ashore to serve one month in a Naval prison; just before we were due to sail we watched silently as a Naval truck and a five man escort in white belts and gaiters drew up alongside and took poor Fred, along with his bag and hammock, off to serve his sentence.

"At least, he'll be safe and sound this time next month,"

muttered Chopper, standing watching beside me, "Christ knows if we will be."

He had something there I supposed. But I knew where I would rather be.

Chapter Eight

Cruising quietly southwards at the head of a large convoy, with the warmer weather helping to lift our spirits, I thought of poor Fred back among the snow of home. What kind of a cell would he be spending his time in, I wondered? I doubted if he would dare tell Ruth where he was, even if he was allowed to write. He would be free before we got back home. I bristled at the thought he might take both girls out, just as I had. But would he kiss Madge on her forehead? Not if I knew Fred, he wouldn't. She would think he had six hands.

From the crow's nest at the mast head I looked back at the ship's in the convoy. One of them was the *Philocoties*, which meant nothing to me then, but to countless thousands of Naval ratings was to become known as the "Flock o' Fleas," which along with the *Edinburgh Castle*, were the base ships in Freetown, West Africa.

There was a disturbance in the sea ahead and from my vantage point I was able to look down on a dead whale surrounded by thrashing sharks tearing lumps out of it.

I watched it wash astern, then swung my binoculars ahead and searched the horizon. There was the occasional white flash of breaking seas, but far out there on the starboard bow was something else that held my glasses. I caught my breath and looked again. I knew I had a reputation for being keen eyed, for no other reason, I assure you, than that there was something there to be seen when I looked. I peered over the canvas dodger of the crow's nest at the deck below. Men in whites were strolling about, some were sunbathing. The bridge lookouts seemed as dopy as usual. All was peaceful.

"Oh Gawd," I whispered to myself, "here we go again!"

I climbed up to the yard arm and stood there with my arm around the mast, trying to find it again. God Forgive me, but down below, everyone, knowing who was up there, were on their feet, staring up at me; after about ten seconds to decide, there was no other report I could give.

"Bridge. Masthead. Submarine bearing green one five!"

No one questioned that report. As I slid down the mast ladder I could hear the alarm bells ringing and watertight doors slamming throughout the ship; the whine of the turbines were increasing rapidly in answer to the full ahead signals.

For several long minutes, no one could see the thing and several curious glances were directed at me as we hurtled headlong towards nothing and away from our convoy.

Suddenly, everyone could see it. It lay there, black, stopped, silent. I don't know what kind of watch they were keeping, but they had no idea we were approaching. Then they saw us. It began to move and our 4.7s commenced firing.

In what seemed like seconds, only its conning tower was still visible and the second salvoe seemed to send spouts of water up all round it; then it was gone and we were attacking an echo.

Pattern after pattern we laid down as we dogged that submarine. All through the night we followed it and well into the next day. But then, after searching all afternoon without once making contact, we had to leave and go after our convoy, now fifteen hours ahead of us.

Closing the land from far out to the westwards, just two days from Gibraltar, a single aircraft approached the convoy. Four engines, possibly a Focke-Wulf, but not with German markings. A single shot from A gun, aimed well ahead, and not at it, caused it to veer away.

A Portuguese mail plane, we decided, from the Azores to the mainland, behaving stupidly. At action stations, we watched it circle. Then it turned for the convoy at full throttle and the fire bells ordered, "Hit it!"

It dropped one single bomb into the sea from a mass of anti aircraft fire before turning away towards the land.

We vowed right there that from now on anything that wasn't British had better keep their distance.

Gibraltar, for the eighth time, looked just as exciting as it did when first we saw it. We tied up alongside one of our sister ships, HMS *Folkstone*. If I had known what was to come, I might have looked much more closely at her than I did.

We seemed to have arrived at the wrong time. Gib seemed to be short of ships. They gave us just one day to rest, then ordered us out to patrol the Straights; a boring job as we were within sight of the Rock all the time and no one would dare use the Straights of Gibraltar without the permission of the mighty Rock, or so we thought.

I don't know who was more surprised when one afternoon, investigating a contact and after inspecting it for a while, decided to drop a few depth charges on it and a submarine surfaced, making hell for leather towards Tangier in Morocco. At full speed, with A gun firing as fast as the crew could reload, we chased after it as it fled for the safety of neutral Tangier, with spouts of water from our exploding shells cascading down on the casing.

We danced with rage and frustration as we had to turn back, nearly in the harbour by now, to observe the three mile limit that was in force.

After four days of patroling the Straights, we were relieved by another sloop and returned to harbour to buy all we could afford of chocolates, scents and silks to bribe our girls back home to do things their mothers had told them not to.

Although cigarettes in our Naafi canteen were duty free they still felt expensive to us. A better bargain, we felt, was the half pound tins of tobacco we bought from the ship's stores once a week. Most of us went around the ship carrying these tins with us, with our name scratched on the lid in case we forgot where we left it.

Like in all walks of life, we had our share of scroungers who never had their tins with them and would reach for yours or whoever's was nearest to them. You soon got to know who they were, and members of the depth charge party devised a way of putting a stop to their little gallop.

The cordite cartridge's for the throwers were kept in a watertight locker close to where they were wanted. They were about the size of a torch but packed enough punch to hurl a heavy depth charge and it's carrier well away from the ship. We used to extract a single strip of cordite from one of these charges. No one would notice and it would have precious little effect on the power. We would cut this strip into lengths, each about half as long as a cigarette, then roll it with the tobacco into a cigarette. So each of our tins usually had three ready made fags waiting for any unsuspecting cadger to take one.

It was great fun during the day waiting for a cadged fag to suddenly burst into flame, but we wouldn't do that during the night, as it was almost as illuminating as a star shell. It cured the cadgers but it would often catch one of us as well when we forgot about the prepared fag.

By sheer bad luck, because of the position in the box, it seemed we were all using the same cartridge each time we played that trick, but none of us were aware of this until that cartridge was loaded and fired during an attack. Instead of the expected face burning bang when the firing pin was pulled, all we got was a dull thud. Before our horrified stares, the carrier just wobbled it's way out of the barrel of the thrower and the thing dropped lazily over the side of the speeding ship.

We, the guilty ones, knew instantly what had caused it, but didn't dare say. No harm had been done; the depth charge exploded and at the correct depth, but not quite in the position it was meant to.

Because of the increasing danger of air attacks, we were now taking our convoys further and further out into the vast Atlantic Ocean. After leaving port we would head out westwards for day after day for a whole week before turning northwards. Then a week later, we would turn inwards for home and tip-toe through the danger zone with no smoke, please, from our charges and maintaining radio silence.

Sometimes we would complete a journey without having to drop a single depth charge or fire a single gun. But as the months went by, trips like that were becoming rarer. From the small world that we could see from the lookout points of HMS *Wellington*, our Britain seemed to be suffering grievous blows that was going beyond our power to avert.

We needed an aircraft carrier with every one of our convoys to fight off the things that were picking us off. But of course, we didn't have them. In our small minds they were all sunbathing down in Gib or swanning about out in Singapore. We just had to keep on wearing our lifebelts and go on picking up the survivors that were left after each attack. The gaps in the lines of ships would disappear as they closed up the ranks, and if you couldn't count you could fool yourself that all was well as line after line of ships plodded on, trusting in God and you to see them through. But you, unlike God, just wasn't good enough to keep them safe.

In Liverpool Bay, as the incoming convoy formed up to negotiate the swept channel, the weather-beaten ships of the escort formed up into line ahead and made back towards the North Channel. After a night of hunting off Rathlin Island, we headed in daylight past Magilligan Point, and made as if on a collision course for the boom defence vessels guarding Lough Foyle. As tugs opened the nets, the five ships that made up the

52nd Escort Group entered the Lough and made for the huge oil tanker anchored in the middle. For better or for worse, this was to be our new base, as far to the westwards as we could afford to be to outreach the forces that were gathering to defeat us. There were places in Ireland that were further westwards that were denied to us, but Ireland had its reasons. We settled for Lough Foyle and the river Foyle that was the sea highway to the City of Londonderry.

It was goodbye to the Clyde. Greenock and Gourock had become almost like home to us. The train service between Glasgow and the south was as familiar to us as the magazines around our gun supports. The camp beds in the basements of Crew railway station were almost as comfortable as our hammocks, and we were almost on first name terms with the ladies in the WVS canteen outside Carlisle station.

I thought about Madge for a long time. If the powers that be had left us in the Clyde, I could have been content to spend the rest of my life with Madge. But wartime had intervened. Who knew what the future held for either of us? HMS *Wellington* could have disappeared without trace within a week, except for that telegram from the Admiralty, like so many dozens of others. Remember them? "The Admiralty regrets that HMS So and So, has been lost on active service. There were no survivors."

From the land to the northwards, small boats began approaching and as our life-giving fuel oil gurgled into the tanks and our unbeatable GPO emptied the sacks of mail onto our decks, we stared with astonishment at the butter and eggs that were on sale in the small boats now coming alongside from Moville, in the Irish Republic.

Unable to resist, like everyone else aboard, I bought five dozen fresh eggs and ten pounds of butter And managed to carry them all the way home to mother in South Wales, along with six tins of corned beef, salvaged from a life boat from one of our sunken ships.

Steaming in line ahead up the River Foyle, the *Wellington* led the way with her crew in the rig of the day lined up on the forecastle and quarterdeck. With the other ships following behind, the 52nd Escort Group came round that last sharp bend and made for their berth alongside the wall at the City of Londonderry. Before we broke ranks to man wires and fenders we noted a Naval truck waiting on the dockside, and there was Fred, trying to keep his hammock off the wet floor. He waved, but no one waved back. We were still under the part of ship routine until the order was given to fall out for coming alongside.

He looked much thinner than when last I had seen him. After we had tied up I helped him carry his kit aboard and we shook hands silently.

"What was your cell like?" I asked him. "Did it have all the mod cons, shower and so on?"

"Cell? asked Fred, startled. "Is that what you all thought? They sent me to a bloody trawler patrolling up off Iceland. Yesterday was the first time I've been ashore in six weeks."

I grinned. Somehow the trials that we had been through these last few weeks seemed less dangerous now; this poor sod had escaped nothing. Trust the Navy to fit the punishment to the crime.

This time it was our turn for boiler cleaning leave. With no sign of any opposition from the Customs, we proudly carried our butter, eggs, sugar and corned beef along with cigarettes, from the railway station at Londonderry to Larne, then by ferry from Larne to Stranraer. It was a long journey from Stranraer, through Glasgow to Carlisle and Crewe and on to Cardiff, but I didn't even crack one of those five dozen eggs.

There were precious few telephones in those days; we would send telegrams if we had the chance but they caused so much apprehension that we hesitated to use them. Being single, if not fancy free, I preferred to turn up on the doorstep and wait for mum to open the door in answer to my knock.

After the tears and the kisses would come the excitement of opening my suitcases and showing the treasures I had brought.

Before I learnt how to darn I would bring as many as ten pairs of socks home with tiny holes in each of them for mum to darn and give to my brother, as I would have long since bought new ones from the ship's store without having to bother about clothing coupons.

She was always amazed at how white my underclothes were, not realising that we would probably buy new ones almost every month. I have mentioned how spotless everyone kept themselves. Once, after a night of passion ashore, one of our mess members had not taken the chance quickly enough of showering and changing; we knew what he had been up to, we could smell him.

I was at a loss being home on leave this time. Sue was in Croydon, and all my mates were away in the forces. Perhaps Fred and I should have gone to Glasgow for a week before going home, or to Liverpool, or to Sheerness. I realised how this was broadening my horizon. From the confines of the Rhondda Valley, never travelling beyond Cardiff, now I could talk knowledgeably of cities throughout the Kingdom. Surely, when peace and sanity was restored to my world, things could never be the same again.

With crew members of the *Wellington* coming from Swansea and Neath and meeting with others at Cardiff, it looked like we would have a compartment to ourselves on the night train to Crew. A few minutes before our train was due to pull out, the train from London pulled in on the opposite platform and I found myself staring at Sue preparing to get out.

I called out to her, startling my shipmates. She heard me and for a moment we stared at each other through two windows.

Believing that I had several minutes to spare, I raced out of the compartment, down the steps and up to the next platform, just as Sue was staring around her after alighting from her train, and already it was pulling out for Bridgend and Swansea. I saw nothing except her open arms; then her lips were fast on mine and her closed eyes held a promise that had no place in a chance wartime meeting on a cold railway platform.

In full view now of the sailors in the other train who were calling urgently for me to join them, I kissed the tears on her cheeks.

"Tom?" I asked.

She held my face in both her hands, then pulled me to her. And the train on the other platform began to move. The yells and shouts from my shipmates galvanised me into action. With a last squeeze of her lovely body against mine, I raced away, down those steps that are still there and up onto the platform after that departing train.

Great Western Railway had a little more than efficiency going for it that night. For no reason, except that the driver and fireman had been watching me kissing Sue and had seen my frantic dash, that massive steam engine braked, and Taff Griffiths from Neath held the carriage door open, while Jonesy, from Seven Sisters, stood on the running board as I raced along the platform. I was hauled into the compartment too late to wave goodbye, to face a barrage of questions. Who was she? Was it serious? She seemed a right smasher from where they were looking. Did I want a whip round to raise the money to bring her to Londonderry so they could all have a better look at her?

I bridled at that suggestion. The thought of this lot looking at her with what they had in mind was hurtful. She was something special. If only there had been more time to ask her about all the things that had been tumbling through my mind. I smiled to myself as I remembered the kisses behind the sports shed in the corner of the playground at school, and the woods when we were older when she clouted me for being too forward.

But those days were worlds away; I had no right to dwell on such things. Already, many of my school mates had been posted as missing. But all the bad things happened to other ships, not to yours. We were just young men, with young men's thoughts and young men's hopes. A home of our own, kids to raise who looked like us, who would walk along streets with lights on. And girls to chase; oh yes, plenty of girls.

I put Sue and South Wales behind me and fended off the questions from my friends as we settled back for the journey to Crewe. Others of our ships company joined us there and soon there was enough to fill several compartments; we waited for the connection to Glasgow and Stranraer in a severe air attack on the terminus. There was always tea and rolls available at Crew and also a WVS canteen just outside the station that I never saw closed.

Suitably refreshed, we huddled in the basement as the place shook from near misses. All the camp beds were occupied, but I was always a bit uneasy about those, not sure whether they belonged to someone or for the use of anybody. We contented ourselves with shouting "Fire!" at decent intervals, and as everyone jumped up, we would look around as well. We made sure nobody got any sleep.

Air raid or not, our train was dead on time. As it pulled out of Crewe station heading northwards, we looked back from the blacked out carriage windows at the glow of fires reflected from the clouds over Crewe and watched the anti aircraft shells bursting in the sky. Royal Navy buses were waiting for the train at Londonderry station to convey us back to the ships. Warships were lined up along the wall, four or sometimes five deep. Cranes, welding sets, riveter's and cables snaked along the dock side and over ships. Armed sentries, in white belts and gaiters, rifles slung over their shoulders, patrolled the dockside along the length of their ship. As we got out of the buses we had to dodge the lorries trundling by with stores and provisions.

Whatever Londonderry was before, it was a Naval base now and the people quickly made us feel at home. While the ships were being made ready for sea we explored our new city. On the very first afternoon, while coming out of Woolworths, I clumsily managed to knock a basket out of a young lady's hand as I came through the door, and most of the contents spilled to the floor. As we gathered them up, I saw a book that she had missed. It was the last thing left and I reached for it before she could.

She snatched it out of my hand, tossed her head, glared at me and walked off into the store. Tongue in cheek, I watched her walk away. Just before she rounded the corner she looked back and saw me watching. If pretty girls can spit in disgust, that's exactly what I thought she was doing as she went out of sight.

There was still a packet of hair grips or something under my shoe and I waited until she was well out of sight before I picked it up. Holding it in my hand as if it was a dirty nappy, I went into the store after her. A moment later I saw her coming back towards me. She could hardly fail to see what I was holding and she stopped in front of me and smiled up at me. She certainly wasn't spitting this time.

We walked back towards the door while I admired her long dark hair laying back over her shoulders. Her blouse was low cut; from where I was standing I could see the lace that edged her bra. She saw me looking, blushed and pulled the neck closer together. We reached the door, still side by side and I pushed away at the damned thing for several long seconds before I noticed the sign on it that said "pull".

Out on the pavement she looked up at me, her grey eyes smiling.

"Are you going to give them back to me or have you a use for them?" There was a lovely Irish lilt in her voice. She was holding her hand out for her hair grips.

"Oh!" I had been staring at her and forgotten I had them. Sheerness, Glasgow, South Wales; they all belonged to another world. Here was an Irish miss laughing up at me and leaving me breathless. I pushed my cap to the back of my head so that my face could be nearer, and a patrol from the *Folkstone* pounced.

It was our own fault; I suppose we had been rough on them in Gib. I was standing there with my cap on the back of my head, one of the things a patrol would be watching for. They were perfectly within their rights. My charmer backed away, and by the time it had been sorted out she was no longer there.

I searched the length of the road, but I couldn't find her and I didn't even know her name. I growled to myself as I walked along. What a moment for a patrol to strike, but it was still marvellous how a pretty girl could make any place look much better. She was pretty enough to have every sailor she passed look after her.

Someone tapped me on the shoulder, and with a start I realised there was another patrol standing watching me, but this one was from the *Wellington*. Jonesy, one of our Leading Seamen, in belts and gaiters said "Message from Chopper. He'll see you in the Fiddlers. And put your bloody cap on straight before somebody see's you."

My shipmates marched off up the road. I would much rather have seen my Woolworth stunner than Chopper anytime, but in the best Naval tradition I asked the first pretty girl that came along where was the Fiddlers. Her eyes started on the bow of my cap badge ribbon, descended slowly to my white lanyard, to the bottom of my tunic, on down to my bell bottoms and over my polished shoes from Bernards, the Naval tailors, as the Navy refused to supply us with anything but boots. It was like as if I had been undressed and felt wanting. I watched her walk away. Ah well! There was always Chopper waiting in the Fiddlers, if I ever found it.

For no reason that we could see, the 52nd Escort Group was ordered out into the Irish Sea for exercises. We pretended that one of the group had broken down and had to be towed. Bags of nothing were passed between ships, and sometimes men were given a ride in a Bosun's Chair or Breeches Buoy between speeding warships. Imaginary oil fuel lines were passed and Away Lifeboats Crew, or Away Number One Boarding Party, or Away Seaboats Crew was practised. Fire Stations and Collision Stations all had their turn. About the only thing that wasn't practised was Abandon Ship; none of us could see the need to be clever about that one. We all had our Abandon Ship stations of course; mine was the second Carley float. We couldn't see the need to practise that.

To reach the upper deck from the forward mess deck, if ever the ship was sinking after being hit, would have meant a perilous journey back to the first exit. That was something you did not dare think about or it would keep you awake at night. That happened to other ships, not to yours.

On one of those evenings, during those exercises, five warships sprinkled smoke floats along mile after mile of the Southern Irish Sea. They travelled flat out and at three minute intervals dropping smoke generators that laid a wall of impenetrable smoke that no German consular officials that might have been watching could possibly penetrate. A huge convoy, bound for North Africa and passing southwards about then was no concern of ours. We were only exercising.

Next morning, the 52nd Escort Group, consisting of five ships, paid a courtesy visit to the town of Larne and were given shore leave for the afternoon. The girls that waved goodbye to us from the waterfront that evening, as our boats took us back to our ships at anchor just off the town, had real tears coursing down their cheeks as they watched their boys in blue being taken away. The duty boats' crews warned they had orders to shoot if anyone jumped off and tried to swim back.

We never did get to see Larne again, except the railway station when passing through.

CHAPTER NINE

Southwards again and through shimmering heat, with the blue sea turning brown with silt from the river as we steamed towards the low, dark line of trees in the distance that was the coast of West Africa. The Grain Coast, the Ivory Coast, the Gold Coast, the Slave Coast. None of which mattered much to us, but we didn't fancy the other name for it, the White Man's Grave. If the heat was anything to go by, it was no wonder. It was far too hot to walk on our deck without shoes on.

The trees opened up to reveal the mouth of a river with thick jungle on either side with an occasional group of small huts. Small craft with big sails crossed from side to side and their black crews waved to us or stared curiously. Then ahead, the river seemed to widen and there were the base ships we had been told to expect, the *Edinburgh Castle* and the *Philocoties*, secured head to stern, close to the right hand side of the river. Just inshore of them was a small pier we came to know as King Tom Jetty. There was no shore installations that we could see, and the group of ships came to anchor.

The way in which a warship came to anchor was an unfailing sign of what sort of ship she was, and it would be watched with interest by all in sight. She would, or should, arrive with all her upper deck crew dressed in spotless whites and standing at ease in lines on the forecastle and quarterdeck. Passing other warships, the lines would be called to attention; bugles or pipes would sound and salutes exchanged. No one could be seen moving on the upper deck, but a lot of work had gone on before this stage was reached.

Out of sight, but ready to move as soon as the anchor was let go, would be a group waiting to lower the gangway, and others ready to swing out the boom for the ship's boats to secure to. Within minutes of the anchor splashing into the water, the boats would be down and ready to go, the boom swung out and rigged for them to tie up on, and the gangway down ready for the Captain or ship's postman to lordly descend to go ashore. No one on any of the other ships would applaud, but let any of those operations go wrong and you could almost feel the howls of derision.

Below decks it was stifling, and portholes were open all along the sides. We watched the busy small boat traffic in the river. There was a constant stream of boats arriving and leaving the two base ships. To take the heat of the sun off the decks awnings were rigged fore and aft. For a brief while it was easy to imagine what the Navy must have been like in peace times when paying courtesy visits to foreign parts, with warm tropical nights, the ship's band playing under the awnings, glasses tinkling, ladies dancing.

We had the awnings and we had a mouth-organ, and it wasn't just warm, it was scorching hot. We didn't have any ladies either, with not much prospects of getting any. Before shore leave was piped, the ship's doctor wanted a word with the crew, so clear lower deck was piped and we all mustered on the quarterdeck to hear what he had to tell us.

From now on, every man aboard would swallow one Mepacrine tablet a day for as long as we remained in the tropics. Everyone should make full use of the iced water tank on the Stoker's mess deck and drink at least one glass full of lime juice that would be provided.

"Glass!" we snorted. "Who was he trying to kid?" Jam pot full, or mug would have made it more realistic.

Then he shook his finger at us as he got to a more interesting topic. "And leave the ladies alone. Remember, this is Africa. If you must be stupid, then wear one of these." And he waved a French letter over his head. "You can get them for free from Doc in the sick bay."

We stared at each other. That was the first time we knew where we could get them. The times we had walked up and down in front of chemist's shops trying to gather courage to go in. Only Dagworth had been brave enough, and only then after we had pushed him through the door, and he came out with a jar of unwanted Brylcream and a packet of aspirins as well.

Our doctor finished his lecture with a warning that had each of us reaching deep into his pockets with protective concern. "If you don't use one of these," waving his French letter in front of his nose, "then don't come to me if it drops off in the night."

Thoroughly frightened, armed discreetly with our protective rubber armour, we lined up for shore leave wearing our white topees, white shirts and shorts. Our own boats took us to the King Tom Jetty and then we were on our own, half expecting to be eaten by lions with every step.

We loved the markets with such strange fruit and vegetables. Yams looked frightening but the bananas! They had long since disappeared from our home shops and we all bought masses of them. There were native bars along the Main Street selling bottled beer, and there was an open air cinema. But the Navy had decided that if we were to be eaten alive by mosquitoes, then it had better be on board the ships; we had to be back aboard by six pm in time for supper. Time enough for us to find out where the most interesting streets and houses were to visit next time ashore.

There was a good bathing beach seawards of the town and the Navy provided buses every half hour from King Tom Jetty to this beach. They also built a small canteen there, selling ice cold beer. So we could spend an innocent afternoon on the beach sunbathing, drinking, surfing and by closing time, nearly drowning.

There were film shows each evening on the *Edinburgh Castle* and sometimes even an ENSA performance. I never saw any real females dancing on the *Edinburgh Castle*, only pretending ones, and they never had the same effect on anyone that I knew.

There were football fields built out towards the beach and, like true Brits and Mad Dogs, the matches between ships were played during the heat of the afternoon.

At night, most of the crew tried sleeping in the cool of the upper deck. Mosquito nets were things we had heard about but never seen. The yellow Mepacrine tablets, which was in place of Quinine, was the only defence we had against Malaria. After a while the tablets turned your skin yellow, so you could tell someone who had been long ashore in West Africa by his yellow appearance. It never had the time to turn any of us yellow as we were seldom there for long enough.

Everyone took turns at being duty boat's crew. One day, coming back from King Tom Jetty to the *Wellington* after landing a boat full of libertymen, I saw smoke coming from two MTBs (motor torpedo boats) anchored close in shore. Soon fire broke out along their stern and I turned our boat towards them to give help.

Two minutes ahead of me was one of the duty trot boats with a black crew, and just as they were going alongside, the depth charges must have exploded. Everything disappeared in flame and smoke and the heat singed our hair. A tidal wave nearly capsized us, and the noise was heard all over Freetown. There was nothing left there for us to pick up a couple of minutes later.

A duty shore patrol usually consisted of a Leading Seaman and four men. "Easy Street," we were told. "That's the one where you turn right at the church. Number four. Go in and make sure none of our boys are in there. It's out of bounds."

We soon found Easy Street. That was the one everybody seemed to be making for. Seeing us standing looking at them, they hurriedly walked on.

After fidgeting uncomfortably for a while, we thought we had better make sure there was nobody inside Number Four. The front door looked as if it had been knocked down a few times before and opened at a touch. There were three rooms inside opening off a passage, and in the one I looked in there was a couple locked in an embrace on a large bed.

I gleefully thumped his backside with my stick, then hastily backed out with muttered apologises as a black man leapt out of bed rubbing his rump.

Chopper, another member of the patrol, seemed to be having better luck than me in the next room. Standing naked and sheepy was Geordy, one of our shipmates, while a black maiden heaped curses on our heads. We fondly clapped him on his bare bottom as a French letter dropped to the floor, then gave him a ticket to prove we had done our duty. Doc would have been proud of him.

We were chased out of there by seven angry females; they threw everything they were wearing at us. Not content with doing it indoors, they followed us out onto the street, much to the delight of the sailors who seemed to be gathering out there. We beat a hasty retreat towards the church.

"Jesus!" gasped Scouse, as he dodged a well flung flimsy dress. "They've got white hair round their minges!"

A shoe whizzed past Chopper's face. "That's talcum power, you nit. They've gotta have sommat to keep the sweat down." We were getting up a right rate of knots by then.

"To hell with Easy Street!" growled our Leading Seaman, as we reached the church. "We'll guard this place instead. We'll make sure none of the dirty swines get's in here." We had a peaceful afternoon.

Early next morning, with the smell of wood smoke from cooking fires drifting over the river and the heat of a new day shimmering the distant trees, hoses were rigged to wash away the mud as cables were shortened. Winches could be heard clanking from several of the ships. Heat shimmered over funnels, and wisps of steam from sirens rose straight up in the still air. Boats were being hoisted and griped in, gangways and booms had gone and the warships waited sleekly for the signal to move out. Then flags fluttered aloft from the signal deck abaft the bridge, answering pendants from the others. The last of the cables were heaved in and ships began to move. Little white waves formed around the bows as the ships of the group began stemming the tide of the river and shifting into the Flotilla formation. Crew members, who last night were drunken young men exploring the whore houses, were now disciplined sailors in immaculate whites standing motionless in lines ready to exchange salutes.

From the *Edinburgh Castle* a bugle call brought everyone to attention, and the base ships were saluted as the group slid by; then we were well on our way into a hostile ocean, and three weeks of convoy protection that no gipsy would risk trying to foretell the outcome.

To those engaged in the horror that was the Western Approaches there was no more welcoming sight than the two arms that was the land on each side of the North Channel. We were nearly home.

Salt rimmed eyes, low on ammunition and ready to sleep standing up, we would count the ships that followed us into the safety of the Clyde or the Mersey. There would be many missing from the number we had started out with, each one of them would have been filled with valuable cargo that the U.K. so desperately needed. And there were always the men who had manned those ships, most of them missing without trace, with only a brilliant flash in the night to mark where they had died.

We always searched astern on the following morning. No survivors ever died because HMS *Wellington* was too afraid to stop to pick them up.

We would tend the injured, sometimes bury at sea those that

didn't survive, but mostly transfer them to other ships in the convoy which could deal with them better than we could. We would watch them safely through the boom defence vessels, then head back through the Irish Sea for Lough Foyle.

The butter and eggs on sale from the bum boats coming from Moville were now a regular routine, and we used this supply to top up our mess rations. Sausages, chips and two eggs for supper was a welcome perk for working out of Ireland, though at no time did we get as far as boiled eggs for breakfast; there was still never the time.

The 52nd Escort Group was to provide the guard of honour for the Duke of Conought, who providentially was to visit the cathedral during the time we were in harbour. With white belts and gaiters and fixed bayonets, everyone that could be spared from the ships marched up and down the dock side with Petty Officers and gunnery instructors quickly bringing us back from lifebelts, duffle coats, and seaboots, to blancoed gaiters, burnished bayonets, chinstraps and polished boots. Gunnery instructors, with their frightening steel whistles and chains and jutting chins that would stop a battleship, had us marching with stamping feet, heads held high and arms reaching for the sky. We dented the concrete with our brass rifle butts. The way we presented arms should have the Duke leaping for the protection of his car.

When they thought we were ready for the public to see us, we marched out of the dockside and into the main street of Londonderry with a Marine band at the head. All traffic was stopped and the pavements were packed with people; as we were put through our paces to show everyone what we could do when pressed, I saw my Woolworth stunner standing not six feet away from me, eyes wide open and her hand half held out towards me.

I was half a second late in sloping arms, and was rewarded with the hot breath and tinkling chain of a G.I. standing behind me. His whispered words were for me alone and would normally have turned my ears red, but I had eyes only for my stunner. There was no way I could have spoken to her. I had to stamp and turn and throw that rifle about as if I was enjoying it. As we marched off down the road I didn't even dare look towards her. As we turned off the main road and marched towards the dockside everyone relaxed; I dared to glance sideways, and there she was, walking on the pavement alongside us.

There was barbed wire and sentries preventing anyone reaching the dock wall, but just before we reached them, I dared a quick glance to call "Woolworths, seven o'clock." And was immediately rewarded with that time honoured shout, "That man there! Take his name!"

No one knew who he was shouting about; it just sounded good. No one took any names either, but it looked like I had a date with my smasher at last.

Later that afternoon, as we changed into number ones ready for shore leave, I knew this was going to be awkward; half the ship's company had heard me make that date, and I was quite sure that half the ship's company intended to turn up for it. Wherever I took smasher, twenty or so sailors with nothing better to do would accompany us. She might enjoy it. But I knew I wouldn't.

Our Chief Petty Officer Stores, Jack Dusty to all of us, had a typewriter in his office. I scribbled a note, altered it, added a word or two, and when it looked right, sauntered down to Jack's office on the deck below.

Dependable Jack was there, just as he always was, counting his stacks of uniform. I had never seen a typewriter, except from a distance, and they looked fearsome enough even from the doorway. He looked up as I gave him the note.

"Print that for me Chief. In big capitals."

He hunted for a plain sheet of paper and never even asked why. "You sneaked in here when I was out and did this yourself, remember," he told me.

I took the letter and from the doorway, "Thanks, Chief. I owe you one."

A letter stuck to the diving store excited a lot of comment. "There will be half price drinks in the Fiddlers tonight at seven o'clock and Miss Maisy Bigger will demonstrate what can be done with a bottle of Guinness."

I believe they had a great night in the Fiddlers. The Landlord said he would try and get a notice like that printed every night, and they had four women claiming to be Miss Bigger.

Me, I was waiting outside Woolworths and there wasn't a sailor in sight that I knew. I was early and walked slowly up and down like the after guard pacing round 'B' gun. After a while I caught myself wondering what Miss Bigger could do with a bottle of Guinness. Then I saw my smasher and stopped to watch as she came along the pavement. She had on a long brown coat with a turned up collar and a wide belt with a big buckle. I realised that I hadn't been wrong those other times. She was pretty. And shapely too; the long coat did nothing to hide that.

I took her outstretched hand. "Miss Bigge . . ." Dammit! I had that woman on the brain! I was still holding her hand.

"Miss who?" She was looking at me, puzzled.

I hastily brushed her question aside. "I haven't been able to sleep at nights for weeks. I've had the fleet searching all of Londonderry for you since you ran away. And I don't even know your name."

"I'm Kate," she said simply, "or Katy if you like." And I grinned at her. Somehow her name fitted her.

"Take my arm, Katy. I'm getting a bit fed up with the doors of Woolworth. And we'll walk up this way." I was half expecting an exodus to come charging angrily from the direction of the Fiddlers.

We saw a film and held hands in the back row and shared some bars of Naafi chocolate. Then I walked her home over a bridge that crossed the river and she stopped me at the end of a street. It was clear that I was to go no further.

"You can kiss me goodnight," she offered, "but half the street will be watching by now." There was a ghost of a smile on her face.

I dutifully kissed her on the cheek. Even the base Padre would have approved of my actions so far. "I've enjoyed my evening," I told her and I had too; she was good company. "But I dunno when I can see you again. We'll be performing for the Duke tomorrow outside the cathedral, but if you're there, I'll be afraid even to wink to you."

I was holding her hand in full view of anybody in the street who wanted to watch.

"It will have to be Woolworths doors every day about four o'clock in seven or eight weeks' time. You can write to me; I can't tell you where I am, but as long as your letters are not returned, you'll know I got them."

She knew what I meant. We had been in harbour long enough for the ships to be ready for sea again. The dockyards were throwing masses of men into the tasks that were necessary to keep these ships at sea where they were so urgently needed. Time in harbour was as short as four days now, only boiler cleaning would lay them up for a week or more.

She stretched to her full height and kissed me on the mouth. "I'll pray for you." Then she was walking away from me along the street. I watched until she was out of sight in the dark, then walked back.

No one had ever offered to pray for me before.

They hadn't been thrown out of the Fiddlers yet, so I thought I'd look in and walk back with Fred or Chopper. Subby, bleary eyed, came past me with a tray of pints. I took one. After my angelic evening it tasted great. Subby came back with a puzzled look to buy another one.

"Miss Bigger gave a bloody great show," he told me. "The things she did with that bottle!"

I stared at him, then I saw Fred at a table near the window and pushed through towards him. "What's this about Miss Bigger?" I demanded.

"Cor!" Fred enthused. "You should have been here. She did it on this table.

The Landlord was calling time and Fred drank half his pint without stopping.

"Did what?" I pleaded. "What did Miss Bigger do on this table?"

"She had blue knicks on," explained Fred. "She showed us that, she lifted up her dress. Then she took one of these bottles," and he picked up an empty bottle from the table to show me.

"That one?" I made ready to jump back.

"Not this one. It was a full one. She pushed it up under her dress, wriggled a bit, then lifted her dress again and it wasn't there. There was only one place she could have put it." We stared at each other.

"Bloody hell! What chance has mere man got? Only you would be any use to her, Fred. Drink up, lets take your deformity back to the ship." He was well blessed and was well teased about it.

"It's not as big as that", he growled, finishing his drink. "We had a whip round for her; she got quite a cap full."

"Not the only thing she got full. Is that your cap back there? You'll need it to get by our Jaunty."

We went through the usual pantomime of teasing the sentries.

"Halt. Who goes there?"

"Germans!"

"You bastards will get shot one of these nights! Come on, stop mucking about."

Next morning, Naval trucks conveyed the guard of honour up to the cathedral and soon, long lines of armed and belted sailors edged the road, standing motionless. The final act to this demonstration came when one of our shipmates, protesting bitterly and wearing a false beard so none of his friends at home would recognise him on the newsreels or in the papers, gave a last rub to our polished boots. We kept him at it by dirtying them again as soon as he had passed.

When the royal cars arrived we presented arms as immaculately as any guardsmen, but no one had any need for concern; he hardly spared us a glance. Then our arms were loaded into one of the trucks and we joined the crowd in the cathedral for the service.

I hadn't caught a glimpse of Katy, but as we were walking out, there she was, at the back of the church. I stepped out of line to greet her, but did nothing more than lightly shake hands. No one dared to bawl me out inside a cathedral, but many were the curious stares as we stood talking on the pavement as the trucks were loading.

"Goodbye, Katy," I murmured. "I believe there's a ships' dance being organised for when we're next in port. Can I take you?"

She nodded eagerly. "I hoped you'd ask, I had heard about it. Of course you can."

There were yells and shouts from the trucks and I hastily squeezed her hand as I dashed for the nearest one. I always seemed to be dashing away from my girls. One of these days I promised myself, I was going to find one I wouldn't have to gallop away from.

Chapter Ten

The 52nd Escort Group slipped quietly away from their moorings that afternoon, and in line ahead formation negotiated the Foyle, steamed quietly past the oilers in the loch and through the gap in the boom defence.

Burnished steel bayonets were in their scabbards, rifles in their racks, white belts and gaiters back in the stores. Oilskins and seaboots, duffle coats and binoculars had taken their place and the ships quickly settled into their sea routines. The searching ping of the asdic, the wind in the rigging, the rushing of the sea, and the whine of the turbines thrusting you onwards, into the Firth of Clyde and past the Ailsa Craig during the night, onwards beyond Greenock and Gourock until we were stemming the waters of the Clyde. And there they were, coming towards us, our charges for the next few weeks.

There were some big chaps among this lot, and we soon saw that some of them seemed to be full of troops. Soldiers were packed around the guard-rails. Christ! If any of those were to be hit!

Perhaps pre-warned by previous convoys, the escorts began slipping inshore of the troop carriers. As we approached a bend in the river, with the land as near now as it would ever be, soldiers began dropping off the sterns of the troopers.

We had never seen anything like this in our lives. In no time at all there were fifty men in the fast flowing river swimming for the land without a hope in hell of ever getting there.

"Away lifeboats crews," were being called on all of the escorts, and within minutes both our seaboats had been slipped and were in among them. The scrambling nets were cut free. Exhausted swimmers, realising they were getting further and further from the land, were making for the warships. The boats were sweeping them up and bringing them back to the nets. One of the troop ships had already stopped and was lowering a gangway. As our seaboats began ferrying them back, the roar of anger directed at us from that deck above sounded like a foul on Cup Final day.

Dagworth, soaking wet, hanging onto the net over the side, had to put it into words, "I'm bloody glad they're on our side!"

I stared at the land as we recovered our boats. Scotland. We had come to know it and love it and wished we were back. Perhaps, one day we would.

We led our reluctant charges out into the ocean, but not before we had noticed something unusual about one of them. We didn't have our aircraft carrier, but it seemed they had given us a fighter plane. It was sitting there on a ramp, pointing out over the bows of one of the lead ships. It looked a very short ramp to us. We were already outside the range of any fighter planes, so if this one ever managed to take off, where would it go? Nowhere, except into the sea.

During the next few days there were some extreme alteration of courses as the Admiralty steered this convoy around reported danger areas, and there were the usual asdic contacts here and there that would cause them to alter out of the way of a suspected attack.

We were well down south when the bombers found us, and they attacked in exactly the way we had been warned. Our Londonderry base had installed some wonderful training aids, and in the dome teacher it had been hammered into us the way the next bomber attacks would develop. And here it was, right as foretold: six attacking aircraft, each of them a four engined bomber, probably Focke-Wulfs, flying in formation straight along the wake of the ships. Just as the rear escorts opened fire, they would break off and fly away. Except for one. That would go the opposite way, making smoke and losing height. Everyone on every ship would be pointing and shouting.

"He's been hit! He's going in!" And his five mates would be sweeping in from the other side almost unnoticed and unopposed.

LAVINGTON COURT after being torpedoed.

But not this time. We knew they were coming all right. Low on the water, wind from the propellers disturbing the sea they were passing over, flickering flame from their cannon positions. The smash of the 4.7s, the heeling of the ship as she turns to avoid, the cry of the turbines at full speed, the fire bells bringing in the roar of the Oerlikons. The sky becomes a mass of red bursts turning black, among which the aircraft are turning and wheeling. The sea is full of splashes as things fall. There are huge water spouts between the ships as the bombs drop. A burst of flame and a pall of black smoke from a nearby ship, and she stops and the others have to take evasive action. A warning cry, "Lookout for the fighter!" We haven't time to see if she makes it off that ramp. There are empty magazines to kick away from the Oerlikons, and shells are sliding up for the 4.7s. Here comes the one that was making the smoke. Empty cartridge cases are littering the decks. The 4.7s are belching away continuously, then suddenly it's over. Perhaps they saw the fighter take off. Did she take off? None of us saw it. Two ships are on fire, and we race towards the nearest one.

Thank God they're not one of the troopers. There is much to be done, as this could well be only a breathing space: the decks to be cleared of cartridge cases, fresh ammunition from the magazines below deck to the ready use lockers around the guns.

We were fast coming up on the burning ship; it looked like the freighter *Lavington Court*, and we could see her upper deck crew fighting the flames. Boarding parties were ready to leap aboard as we crunched alongside. Within seconds over twenty of our crew had joined them on her deck. Pulling back to avoid too much damage, but not before many of our guard-rails had been wiped away, our hoses poured water into the fires.

The roar of an aircraft engine sent the guns aiming aloft again before the cry of "Don't shoot. It's the fighter!"

We waited spellbound as the bravest man in the fleet circled the ships with nowhere to go except into the sea. We saw the canopy go, then he jumped, and we saw him begin to fall. Nobody breathed until his parachute blossomed white in the blue sky, and one of the corvettes sped to pick him up.

They brought him back to show us: a typical Flying Officer Kite, long handlebar moustache, standing soaking wet in his flying kit, waving to us from the deck as they sped by. The cheers he got in admiration from every ship would last him a lifetime.

We had to get our crew back. There was still a big convoy

plodding onwards. Again both ships crunched together causing more damage as the boarding parties got back aboard. One of the corvettes would stay with her for as long as needed. Before dark, the convoy was back on track, escorts in position.

Trying to help the Lavington Court after she had been torpedoed.

There wasn't much use keeping radio silence now, the attacking aircraft would make sure everyone knew where we were. During the days that followed there were three more air attacks. How we wished that more of our ships could carry fighters! But soon we were having support from Gib. Catalina flying boats were a welcome sight, and tugs rushing by going to the rescue of the still floating casualties were urged on by our shouts.

Gibraltar. A glittering star in the distance sending shimmering light over the Straights. We watched it through tired eyes as our huge convoy slid silently by during the night, and well before dawn the last of our ships were far out of sight into the Mediterranean.

With no more trouble we entered the Bay of Algiers on the

coast of North Africa and, thankfully, dropped anchor after oiling. That night there was a high level air attack. We stood too at the guns for most of the night listening to the frightening sound of falling bombs coming down from a long way up, and you just had to sit there and drink cocoa.

Next day they allowed us to see the harbour and we steamed in alongside one of the troopers we had brought in. She was empty now, and we soon found out why they wanted us. Everywhere you looked there were lines of German and Italian prisoners of war winding their way towards the ships. Armed guards were required to direct them. Once more our rifles came out of the racks and we spent the day guiding them into the transports.

German prisoners of war being embarked at Algiers for the UK.

Next day they gave us shore leave and we found out that Algiers was French. The way the tram cars towing other tram cars clattered their way around had us leaping for our lives. Someone thrust a piece of paper into our hands and the only word that we could understand was exhibition. We thought it meant a circus and innocently looked for the address. Even a couple of our 'Stripeys', and they were supposed to know everything, helped us look for this circus.

Number 46 looked like a large house to us. You paid in any sort of currency at the door. Inside, it was like a very small cinema and almost every seat was filled by someone in uniform. By now our innocence was wearing off and we began to get the idea of what we were getting into.

Right at the front, alongside the ring, we spotted three of our crew, but they hadn't seen us come in. Then suddenly the lights went out and a spot picked up a shapely girl coming gliding in from behind some curtains. She had a tray with three glasses full of something. Our three chums at the front were lit up by the spotlight. Little Geordy, sitting in the middle, was the target for this lovely teaser.

We watched a little breathlessly and wishing we could change places as she danced in front of him, stroking his face, passing her tray of glasses under his nose, leaning over him so that he could see straight down her flimsy bra. Then she took one of the glasses and urged him to drink. And of course the clot did.

Perhaps that was a bit unfair, because at this stage we would willingly have changed places with him. The spotlight changed to red, and with one hand she slipped her bra off and used it to wipe the sweat from Geordy's forehead.

We could see his hands trembling from where we were sitting. After swaying around him for a moment or two, she helped him drink the second glass. With that same one handed movement, off came her pants and she danced there naked, still holding her tray. After a couple more circuits of the ring, she put her tray down and brought that last glass over to Geordy. He started to stand up to meet her but she pushed him back onto his chair, then rubbed her breasts against his face as she helped him swallow that last drink.

We nudged each other, trying to see if there were any vacant seats down where they were. All the action seemed to be going on down there and we yearned to be a part of it.

A richly dressed Arab cracking a whip urged in two more girls dragging something that looked like a guillotine. Ah well, we thought, seeing this was French, guillotines were normal things in this part of the world, but when he started to whip our naked dancing beauty into this contraption, we began to resent it. She appealed for help from our Geordy. After those three drinks he had downed and being right there in the front row from where he was best place to give it, wild horses wouldn't have kept him in his seat.

He shot into the ring. In just two seconds the guillotine turned out to be stocks, and our Geordy was held securely by his head and hands, peering at us like a seagull that had tried to lay an egg in the crow's nest.

The ring was now empty except for poor Geordy. Then two tents swayed into view and after a couple of circuits, two black heads came out of the top and there were two big women prancing in front of the prisoner. The tents began to slip from their shoulders, and in front of our wondrous eyes the biggest breasts we had ever seen began to emerge. How could they walk with things like that weighing them down?

With much banging of drums and clashing of cymbals the tents slipped to the floor and two black females with the biggest knockers we had ever seen gyrated naked in front of our Geordy. The tufts of hair at the bottom of their stomachs was level with his face. It was there to stop dirty devils like us from eating what it protected or so we had often been told. Amid roars of laughter, we watched poor Geordy trying not to put this to the test.

They rubbed nipples in his eyes, bounced boobs on his brow, brushed fannies in his face. Then the lights came on and the Arab released our mate and the three girls cuddled him in the ring as we applauded. We thought we had attended a good exhibition. Next time we would know not to expect a circus. Our education was proceeding normally.

In just three days the transports were ready to leave Algiers. The portholes of the troop carrier we were tied up alongside were full of Italian prisoners, and they tried to talk to us. One asked me by motions for a cigarette. Remembering the ice creams from our Italian friends back home, I handed him half a tin of tobacco and a couple of packets of cigarette papers. They wanted to know where they were going. When we told them to England, we could hear them passing it on around the deck. For most of them it would be on again to Canada after that.

By early afternoon the ships were streaming out of the harbour and forming up for the long voyage home. Temporary repairs had been carried out to the damage sustained by assisting the *Lavington Court*. But not long after clearing the Straights of Gibraltar the Asdic began playing tricks. Sometimes it would work, sometimes it wouldn't, but as soon as the weather began bumping the bottom it packed up altogether. The fault was pinpointed to the aerials in the boot that was bolted to the ship's bottom, and there was no way of reaching that while she was at sea.

There was nothing for it but to run for the nearest port which was neutral Azores, belonging to Portugal. From just off the land we asked for permission to enter harbour to carry out emergency repairs. We were directed to Ponta Delgada. We covered all guns and depth charges as we closed the harbour and we saw that every vantage point was crowded with people watching us coming in.

With lines of sailors standing motionless in white uniforms on the forecastle and quarterdeck, we saluted the signal station, and a guard of honour on the harbour presented arms to our new white ensign fluttering at our stern. Beyond the harbour, in the next dock, we stared in disbelief at the upperworks of a German submarine. We could see some of her crew climbing to high points to look at us.

The British Ambassador and his family arrived by car with the Union Jack flying from the bonnet. We hurried to get our gangway out for them to come aboard. His daughter stopped half way along between ship and shore and she smiled sweetly at us. There was no need for her to walk really, we would gladly have carried her. After they had gone forward to the Captain's cabin, Chopper walked mincingly across the gangway to secure the shore end of it. He stopped half way over and smiled sweetly at us and started to lift up his shirt to show us his belly. Infuriated, we shook it violently, trying to tip him off, but he nipped ashore too quickly.

Small boats were making for us from across the harbour loaded with what looked like green footballs. Our 'Stripeys' took one look and reached for their money. We watched Ginger lower a bucket on a line and haul back one of these footballs and we gathered round him as he pulled out his knife and cut it open. That was the first time most of us had ever seen a water melon. From then on, any spare moments saw us sitting in the sun on the upper deck eating delicious water melons.

Shorty Bates, our diver, was already at work beneath the ship, while welders from the harbour tried to make our missing guard-rails a little less dangerous. Red flags were flying, warning that divers were working, our own boats were down, Yardarm groups (powerful lights) were slung over the side so that work could go on throughout the night.

The Ambassador had brought the news that because of the presence of the German submarine the authorities had asked that no shore leave be given. It made sense of course, but we had to ask, "Were they being given any shore leave?" nodding towards the submarine.

"Of course not!" we were assured. Mollified, we went on enjoying our water melons. We couldn't help but wonder. Which of us had caused the damage that had driven her in here? Would it be worth it if we waited outside the harbour for her to come out?

By noon next day the asdics were working again, and crowds began to gather as the word spread that the British warship was about to leave. A lorry arrived with fresh fruit, bread and pastries, a gift from the town, a lovely gesture, we thought. It was quickly manhandled aboard. Seaboats had been hoisted, wires singled. We blew kisses to the girls who seemed to be pressing close to the edge of the dock wall. They blew kisses back, which proved to all of us that they knew English. In spotless whites, trying not to notice the many watching heads on the German submarine, we waited ready to go. The Ambassador's car was there, hemmed in by the crowd, but we could still see the Union Jack on it. Our brand new white ensign hung proudly at our stern. Then that awful shriek from her siren blasted out over the town, three short blasts, meaning my engines are going astern.

Brown, muddy water was being churned up, wires were quickly let go and run in, dropped on the deck where they were, and hands fell in for leaving harbour, standing motionless, heads held high, longing to, but not daring to blow back the kisses being showered on us. Salutes were exchanged with the signal station as we turned, still inside the harbour. Then a farewell blast on our siren that had all of us gritting our teeth. The wind increasing along the deck as the speed built up with the rising whine of the turbines.

"Fall out, secure wires and fenders. Hands to cruising stations."

We were at sea again. Spotless whites gave way to warmer clothes and you secretly located your lifebelt. A regretful last look at the land fading away behind, who knows, but for that blasted submarine there might have been some new little Britishers to cement the friendship between two countries.

The U.K. bound convoy from Algiers gave us a rousing welcome when we caught up with them. As usual, it was a thin pillar of smoke from one of the stragglers as she strove to catch up that gave us our first sight of their position. The pillar of smoke suddenly thickened as she stoked up the fires when they first caught sight of something astern coming up on them.

With many thousands of prisoners of war on those ships, you would have thought this was one convoy that would get through without opposition. But not so. The bombers were ranging far out into the ocean now. When they found you it was look out, they would return day after day, in groups of four or six, sometimes twice a day, and you knew they would be directing every submarine within range towards your position.

It was not often a submarine would press home a daylight attack; the escorts were well able to deal with that and were deadly dangerous to anything that tried. But coping with air attacks during the day and knowing that submarines were being guided into position ahead for the night attack was a bit stomach churning.

Massive course alterations immediately after dark could throw their calculations out, but it was aircraft we needed to combat the bombers and keep the submarines down to prevent them getting ahead of us and laying in wait. Aircraft that we didn't have.

We slept when we could, where we could. I can remember having a good hour's sleep on the depth charge rails with my lifebelt as a pillow. I awoke to hear Subby reading the log at the stern and telling someone to pull the lever and drop the bastard over the back. I angrily chased him up onto the boat deck, but remembered my lifebelt left on the depth charges and went back for it.

By the time we reached the North Channel we had precious few depth charges left; another day at sea would have seen us taking charges from the supply ship.

This was the day of the ship's dance. In Londonderry our girls would soon be taking our names in vain; we would never get there in time now. The dodging and altering we had been forced to do had added days to our journey.

Ah well, it wouldn't be the first time that female curses had been heaped on our heads. I wondered what Irish curses Katy knew. Pity about that dance. There were plenty of quiet places outside where we could have gone for some fresh air. There would have been no neighbours watching to put the damper on the proceedings.

When two trawlers arrived from ahead of us to take over the convoy we assumed that C in C Western Approaches was pulling his finger out to get the 52nd Escort Group home in time for their dance and accepted it as a hero's due reward. With any luck, we could make it yet, but none of us thought much of negotiating the Foyle in darkness.

We rocked the boom defence vessels by rushing past them too fast and were rewarded by a remonstrating toot toot from a steam whistle. We showed them how to do it by a shattering blast from that damned siren that had even the eggs and butter merchants heading for home. Not even stopping for fuel, we formed into line ahead and steamed up the river. With just enough light to see the town from the last bend, we got to the wall and berthed on each other as the light went.

Naval buses took us off to the dance as soon as we were ready. Never mind about supper, we were told, the Naafi funds have provided all the grub you'll need at the dance. This was getting better and better. We licked our lips. "Er, what about, er . . ."

"Yes, there's a few barrels of beer put on as well." Now we were all for it, couldn't wait. We could hear the band from the buses as we arrived outside, and I began thinking more and more about Katy. Would she be there, but more importantly, would she be there with me? We had been away a long time and Londonderry was full of sailors.

We gave up our hats at the door and went into the hall. There were lots of girls there, many of them dancing together. At the far end, near the stage, a long table with a white cloth held a wonderful selection of plates of food and there was a stack of plates on the end.

At each end of the stage was a barrel of beer and a pile of glasses, half pint glasses we noted with a frown. Shouldering Fred out of the way, I filled a glass and looked around for Katy.

Chopper went gliding by holding a girl close. She snuggled up to him and they danced so perfect that many stopped to watch. It didn't look the same Chopper that had turned the air blue when he hit his finger while mending someone's shoe. Then I saw Katy. She was on the other side of the hall, and she was wearing a sailor suit almost like mine, but with little buttons down the front. She looked much better in it that I did in mine.

She was already looking at me when I saw her and I forgot about the band up there on the stage and all the dancers gliding by. The glass in my hand was suddenly in the way and I thrust it towards the first person that passed in front of me. I walked across that dance floor, not seeing or hearing anyone; it was just Katy, my smasher, coming towards me.

We met in the centre of the floor and I held her hands. I looked into her eyes as her arms slipped around my neck. I didn't want to dance, just to hold her close was enough. Someone bumped into us and a voice whispered "Why don't you marry the girl?" I closed my eyes. Oh, God. At that moment, how I wanted to.

I held her at arm's length. "You're not married yet, then."

She lifted her head to look at me. "Are you glad or sorry about that?" Her soft, Irish brogue twisted my heart. I pulled her close and kissed her hair, smelling her perfume.

"Of course I'm glad. Fancy Londonderry without you!" Chopper tapped me on the shoulder, took her from me and I watched angrily as they moved away. I looked around for the one who had my glass, couldn't find him, so got another. Katy came hurrying back to me and, leaving my glass on the stage with the band, I held her as we circled the floor. I wasn't much of a dancer and envied the way that Chopper was becoming the star of the show.

Supper time, and with my arms around her waist, we waited our turn at the table and then found a place at the side of the room. Afterwards, I took her out into the garden at the side of the hall where we could see over the roofs of the buildings right down to the river glinting in the light of the stars. It was possible to make out the dark shapes of the warships alongside the wall, but the way she was holding me tight was driving all thoughts of warships from my mind. From the safety of some trees behind a seat in the garden I opened some of those buttons on her tunic and slipped my hands round to the catch that held her bra. Her lips found mine just as I released the strap and my hand closed over her breast as we clung together in the dark. Her hands held my face and we could hear the band start up again in the hall after the meal break.

Clouds began covering the stars. As the darkness around us deepened, my hand slipped from her breast to her waist and I could feel the elastic of her knickers as my fingers slid inside. We both seemed to be short of breath and she was clinging so tight to me that there was no room to go any further. I moved my hand back to her breast, holding her tight to me, feeling her nipple under my fingers. I wanted so much to tear her blouse away and bury my face between her warm shoulders, and she had that tantalising way of moving her face from side to side as she kissed me. Unable to contain myself any longer I lowered my hand back to her waist and inside her knickers.

I saw her hand coming as I heard her gasp and they must have heard the sound of the slap in the hall even over the sound of the band. She was standing there, holding her hand over her mouth as I narrowly avoided falling backwards over the seat. We stood there in the darkness of the garden amongst the trees for several long moments as she waited for me to recover. I held my breath, waiting for the uppercut that I surely deserved. She giggled from behind her hand, and I felt the tension slipping from both of us.

Ruefully, I rubbed my face; then I pulled her to me. "Sorry Kate, but I'll go on chasing your charms as long as you look as lovely as you do tonight."

Her arms came back around my neck. "It was my fault," I heard her whisper, "I shouldn't have led you on."

How could she know that the memory of that warm, soft

breast under my hand, and the hope of other delights that she might permit, would torment me so often during those long nights at sea in the North Atlantic? For me, Londonderry would always be Kate, and that dream of every young man of closing the door of a lovely room and gently disrobing his Kate, to reveal all the charms that she had to offer would keep me awake for many a night to come in many different parts of the world. Perhaps one day soon that dream would be a reality. It was something to work for, anyway.

Kate seemed to be having some difficulty in fastening her bra, and it took a real effort on my part to stand idly by and let her do it, when everything in me demanded that I tear it off and bury my face in her breasts. A few moments later, somewhat recovered, but still rather breathless, we hugged each other. Then she pushed me away and, holding hands, we made back to the dance.

There seemed to be more girls than sailors dancing, After a while Katy and I found a seat against the wall. On seats all around the room sailors were fast asleep. Half the glasses near the barrels of beer had not been used. The patrols in belts and gaiters standing near the door had nothing to do. The many days and nights of coming home through the Western Approaches were taking their toll.

Navy buses took our girls home. Katy woke me to whisper, "Woolworths, seven o'clock on Wednesday."

I grinned sleepily. "Sorry, Kate. Wednesday it is." I watched her walk away from me. Those swaying hips had almost made me lose control of my senses.

She could still bring me wide awake even now if only she would turn and beckon. There was stirrings that had no place in a single man's world. She turned at the door and blew me a kiss; then she was gone. And I went back to sleep as we waited for our buses to return and dreamt of what might have happened between me and Kate in a darkened garden.

Next morning, we took HMS *Wellington* back down the river

Foyle to the oilers at Movile, and after filling up, moved out into the North Channel, round Rathlin Island and into Belfast Lough for repairs in the dockyard.

We had never seen Belfast before. It was bigger than Londonderry, but we soon found our way around, and one night went far out along Falls Road in a tram.

Wednesday found me on Quartermaster duty on the gangway in the dockyard in Belfast, and there was no way I could tell Katy in Londonderry not to turn up at Woolworths.

Chapter Eleven

Three days later, with repairs completed, we were heading westwards again, leading another convoy far out into the Atlantic before turning south towards the warmer weather. We were already wearing white clothes before the first of the bombers found us. As the Escorts closed in on the ships we were surprised to see many of them putting up barrage balloons. This was the first time we had ever seen this done at sea.

The pulsating roar of the attacking aircraft seemed to be coming from all directions, but so far none of the ships had opened fire. The *Wellington* was close in to the starboard side of the first column of ships. She was not travelling at full speed or she would have rapidly left the convoy behind. Their speed was eight knots, and some of them were having difficulty in maintaining it.

The attack would come from behind, as the length of a ship was an easier target than the width for the bombs they were armed with. We heard the full ahead signal from the telegraphs in the wheelhouse to the engine room, and the rising scream of the turbines as they drove her forward caused the wind to increase. Then, under full rudder, she turned, heeling over sharply as she came around.

For a moment it looked as if even the boat deck would go under water; then she came upright and was steaming rapidly past ship after ship as she made for the rear of the columns. Turning again, crossing very close to the wake, she came into position almost in the white water behind the last ship and there behind us, was a V formation of eight four engined bombers coming straight for us.

I waited for the firing bells shaking with fear, gasping for breath. No sound, just the soughing of the wind and that calm schoolmasters voice, who couldn't see what was happening anyway, calling the lessening ranges. The rising and falling sound of the aircraft engines got ever louder.

It was at that moment that a hatch on the quarterdeck opened and a head poked through beneath the menacing barrel of the after 4.7, which was just about to commence firing. He was looking aft, and saw nothing of the menace that was behind him, and was obviously relating to those below what was going on. It took a second or two for him to take in what he was seeing, and most of our fear dissipated as we recognised the Duchess. A few seconds from now and he was in for one hell of a shock as B gun smashed off its first clenched fist just above his head.

We heard him yell to those below that they were coming up towards us; then our warning shouts caused him to turn to face forward. At that moment the falling range triggered the response and the after 4.7 smashed off the first round and a heavy explosive time estimated shell smashed towards the oncoming formation.

That first flash of burning cordite caused sunburn like scorches on unprotected flesh dressed in white shirts and shorts, caught once more without their anti-flash helmets and gloves. From now on we would keep them in the ready use ammunition lockers around the guns, instead of the now unreachable lockers beyond the closed water tight doors where we kept our kit.

The V formation of the oncoming aircraft broke up as the black shell-bursts in the sky began barring their progress. We could hear the whine of our turbines decreasing as the *Wellington* sacrificed her speed and safety to stay in their path. The paint on the gun barrels of the turrets was beginning to smoke again as the heat from the burning cartridges which were cascading from the guns began littering her decks. By turning slightly aside, both 4.7s could come to bear on the approaching danger.

The thick leather belt that held me securely into the shoulder clamps of the port Oerlikon kept my face within inches of Donald Duck painted on the inside of the armour plated protection of the gun.

"Wait for it," he kept saying, "wait for it." When I pressed that trigger, there was just eight seconds, and over a hundred shells, with impact nose fuses, every forth one a tracer would be in the air, speeding towards its target. Then the magazine would be empty and the gun's crew would have to snatch it off and put on a new one.

With much practise, it took just seven seconds to change magazines. But what damage could an aircraft do in seven seconds? Donald Duck and his warning finger helped to keep our hands off those triggers until the Open Fire bells close to our ears authorised us to squeeze, but only iron discipline forced us to wait as four-engined horrors came roaring towards us. Kitty's little silver cross swinging on the gun sight helped all of us to stand and wait, which was the most difficult part of all.

The watertight hatch on the quarterdeck had slammed shut, but not before the heat from that first shot had burnt the hair from our Duchess and saved him the cost of a haircut for the next four months.

The formation of attacking aircraft had broken up and the sky over the convoy was a mass of busting shells. I followed one aircraft, pumping short bursts of red tracers straight into her belly. It flew right past a great big silver barrage balloon and my red tracers sliced through it and turned it instantly into yellow flame that sank down onto the ship that was towing it. I bit my lip as I saw the flames; then forgot all about it as I opened fire on the next aircraft coming into my sights.

The sky seemed to be full of shell bursts and crisscrossing tracers. All six aircraft were over the lines of ships; they looked huge as they banked and twisted. One of them went into a sharp turn as it came back towards the rear of the convoy, then banked again to follow up the lines of ships. It seemed to stand on its wing tip, black and menacing in the sky and for that brief moment was within range of every gun on HMS *Wellington* and every gun on the ship was pouring shells into it.

Whether it was seriously damaged, whether the pilot was killed or hurt, or whether he thought he was invincible with the power of those four roaring engines, no one will ever know. Whatever it was, he seemed to have forgotten about those barrage balloons. It roared across in front of us towards the nearest ship on the corner, at not much above mast height, straight into the wire going up to the barrage balloon she was towing.

The starboard wing, along with two still roaring engines, was sliced away from close to the fuselage and went twisting away into the sea. The aircraft seemed to go upwards, then it corkscrewed off to the right and, with her two remaining engines still roaring away like a chicken that is supposed to run without its head, plunged into the sea with an almighty splash clear of all the ships.

The attack on the convoy faltered and they seemed to be reforming into formation out on the port horizon. HMS *Wellington* increased to full ahead and steamed through the spot where the plane had gone in. There was nothing there, not even wreckage.

They went home one short, but they left us with three burning ships and we went to help the nearest one to us, the *Flora McDonald*, burning fiercely from bomb hits forward of her bridge. There was no way to come alongside another ship while at sea without causing damage of some sort, so portholes and guard-rails along our side were being punished again.

It was dark before the mess was cleared enough to resume the journey, and now it would be the turn of the submarines. But there were lifeboats back there behind us, with dead and injured people needing help, so it was full ahead once more heading back the way we had come and all binoculars searching for the boats that we knew full well were there.

SS FLORA McDONALD trying to make Gibralta being towed by a tug after being set on fire by bombers.

It was the cigars they were smoking that we saw first. There were two lifeboats, roped together, and all round the seats we could see the red tips as they drew on their big cigars. We cut the scrambling nets free as we slid towards them, sailors down on the nets ready to drop into the boats to help the injured. Screws churned the sea white as they stopped the *Wellington*.

It wasn't cigars, it was the little red lights on their life-jackets, we all had them, but this was the first time we had seen them in use.

"Put those lights out," we urged. If we had seen them, so could others, and sitting there, stationary, it was a hairy moment.

Everyone on the ship breathed a sigh of relief as the screws began pushing her ahead once more, leaving the empty boats quietly behind as a silent monument to someone's grief.

One of our older Leading Seamen, Scargill from Liverpool, a soft spoken, gentle man, was usually the one who had the task of drawing a bolt of canvas from the ship's stores, and not for the first time had to prepare a body for burial at sea. A wide wooden plank would be pushed out over the lower guard rail, just aft of the starboard whaler, and the body, sewn in canvas, would be placed on the plank with a new White Ensign draped over it. The Bosuns Mate would go round the ship piping, "Clear lower deck. Hands attend funeral service abaft the starboard whaler."

Everyone not on duty would gather there in the rig of the day. Then it would be off caps and the Captain would read the funeral service. The end of the plank would be lifted and the body of that poor seaman would slide from under the ensign and drop into the sea. Sometimes there would have to be more than just one burial.

With the convoy dispersing at Gibraltar, the *Wellington* entered harbour with a fresh breeze helping her along. We could almost feel the cussed mood she was in, and as we stood silently in line dressed in clean whites, we eyed each other apprehensively as we could feel her refusing to answer her helm. The telegraphs seemed to be constantly ringing new orders to the engine-room as the wind blew her ever nearer towards the Cataliner flying boats nodding gently at their moorings, like swan's blissfully unaware that the axe man was coming.

They had flown over us often enough. It seemed that we were soon going to have the chance to look down on them. R.A.F. crew in shirts and shorts working on the aircraft were staring up at us. Those that could swim began diving overboard, and those that couldn't jumped off anyway. Our entering harbour routine broke up as we ran to fend off the wings coming towards us.

No wonder they were jumping. There were bombs slung under some of those wings. I recoiled in fear as I tried to get a fender between a crumpling wing and our ship's side as I saw a bomb come inboard at ankle height. Lifebelts were being thrown overboard at the R.A.F. boys in the water.

When at last we managed to get her stern into the wind and draw away there were six of those flying boats damaged. We tried to look like we damaged Cataliners every day, and told everybody that it wasn't us, it was our sister sloop, the *Folkstone*. We said it so often that even we believed it in the end. On the credit side there were probably a few R.A.F. boys who had been non swimmers before who could swim now.

They didn't give us long ashore at Gib, just enough time to spend all our spare money on silk stockings and perfume for our girls back home. We saw some of the remembered faces from our training division days who were dodging the column we thought, as they sunbathed on the beaches of Gib, while we did all the work and the real dodging, taking the bacon home. The strain on their faces and the way their cigarettes shook as we talked never registered, and it took post war news reels with their pictures of those awful Malta convoys to give me an idea of the strain they must have been under.

In the mountain above Freetown.

We were ordered next to Freetown; we had been sent from Gib to escort a small group of ships – a punishment, we thought, for damaging their flying boats. We stared in disbelief as we came up the river to see warship after warship flying the American flag, at anchor off our base ships. The Yanks were here in force, and there seemed to be hundreds of small boats plying between ships, all flying a small American flag at their stern. This was our first close encounter with our friendly allies.

We were out-numbered a thousand to one. When shore leave was piped there didn't seem to be the usual enthusiasm. But then, common sense prevailed. After all, we were on the same side.

It turned out to be a thoroughly miserable afternoon. Every bar we went in was full of Yanks, and all the laughter and singing stopped the instant we looked through the door. Even the natives were hostile, sensing they had us by the short hairs at last. We were left with that itchy feeling they were about to show us who was boss. Sometimes a sailor or two would come flying out through an open window, and after a quick dust off and without waiting for their caps to be thrown out after them, they would hurry to join the column retreating towards King Tom jetty.

After frantic signals our own boats hurried to take us off as the jetty was proving more dangerous than the street. From the safety of our ship we shook our fists in defiance. We're not afraid; just didn't want to be ashore, that's all.

Next morning, the word was going around. Watch the river. Just like yesterday, the place was full of the Stars and Stripes. But there was a ripple of excitement as we waited for something to happen. And then we gasped. Christ! Look what's coming in.

A powerful British fleet was making their majestic way up the river towards their anchorage. I don't know where they came from or what they were up to, but it was something that took your breath away. Everyone of us who saw it straightened his shoulders with pride. There were massive great battleships, an aircraft carrier, cruisers, along with their destroyer screens. The river was full of grey ships that towered above us, and we seemed to be doing nothing else but standing to attention while pipes and bugles sounded as we exchanged salutes.

We grinned to ourselves at the mess some of them were making of coming to anchor and almost burst out laughing as a destroyer lowering a boat took too many turns off and it dropped into the water leaving its crew hanging in mid air on the lifelines. If the Admiral, or whoever was boss, saw that performance there would be signal flags flying in a minute, and sure enough, a signal hoist went up on one of the battleships. You could almost feel that huge monster shaking with wrath, and just in case he also objected to our working clothes we hurriedly moved out of his view behind the gun turrets.

When shore leave was piped after dinner there was the usual rush to get ready. As the liberty boats came alongside, the Inspecting Officer pointed his finger at us, then looked hopelessly at those poor American ships at anchor, now lost amongst the might of that British fleet. Throwing his hands up in despair, he stood aside to let us go.

Freetown was ours again. Every bar the Yanks dared to look in suddenly went silent as angry faces turned to stare. Out on the street American sailors would come hurtling out of a window and without stopping for their hats, would make a bee line for the jetty, and the black natives would throw stones after them as they went.

Next morning we tried to keep out of the way as that mighty fleet made for the sea. If we fought with the Americans ashore, we saluted them now as they passed us, slotting into position among the fleet that was leaving Freetown. Soon, there were just a small group of warships left in the anchorage, and they were being informed about an ENSA concert on the base ship tonight. It felt strangely safe to see that things were back to normal.

At a football match next day against a team from one of the other escorts, we cheered our Jack Dusty as he dribbled his way through the opposition. We had our bathing suits and towels with us for a few hours on the beach after the match. It was scorching hot and we knew all about mad dogs and Englishmen and noon day sun; as Jack lay on the penalty spot after a tackle we shouted 'Foul' as we waited for him to get up. He never did get up. Our Jack Dusty died right there on that football field, cradled in the arms of dozens of his shipmates.

The letter from his wife was pinned to our notice board. She had lost a husband, she told us, but we had lost a shipmate. How right she was.

Coming alongside HMS Wellington in the ship's Whaler.

As we prepared to leave Freetown next day we saw the biggest ship we were ever likely to see coming up the river. The *Queen Mary* was coming into Freetown. She was big enough to hoist ships the size of HMS *Wellington* up to her davits as lifeboats.

A Signalman was quickly detailed to stand by the halyards of the ensign. No matter how big she was she was still a merchantman and should salute a warship. Trying to look as if he wasn't there, we waited to see what she would do.

She steamed past us like a street of skyscrapers overlooking a semi-detached. We almost needed binoculars to see her Officers up there on the bridge. And meticulously, she dipped her ensign to us as she passed, and the waiting Signalman nipped out of hiding to dip our white ensign in proud reply. We steamed out of Freetown with chests the size of those women we had seen at the exhibitions in Algiers.

HMS *Wellington* was suffering the fate of most of the escorts that were engaged in the battle of the Atlantic. Too long at sea without repairs or dry docking. Repairs put off until next time were mounting up. Weeds and shell fish growing on the metal plates below the water line were cutting her speed. Enemy submarines, as many as six in a pack were laying in wait for the vital supplies we were shepherding home. The massacres this produced when as many as sixty ships ran into them are better forgotten. But they will never be forgotten by the crews who lived in those ships.

C in C Western Approaches assembled all the available crews working out of Londonderry to warn us of the opposing forces that were marshalling against us.

"Sprinkle depth charges all over the Western oceans," he told us. "Sprinkle them like salt on every contact you come across. I will provide you with thousands, and I shall expect you to use thousands. In every convoy I will have a supply ship able to replenish you with all the ammunition you may need. On you and your ships depends the fate of this great country." Far from being proud, it scared the hell out of most of us.

Escorts went to sea like floating arsenals, with their sterns almost under water with the weight of the explosives they carried. Training Division produced in a vast hanger outside Londonderry, the complete quarterdeck of a ship, suspended on compressed air pistons that bounced and heeled over just like a real ship would in rough weather while travelling at speed; crews practised loading throwers and firing them into nets slung along the sides, while important guests and notabilities watched from the safety of a balcony.

Coming home from Africa with a convoy under attack from sea and air, the *Wellington* was caught in the middle of the lines of ships after an air attack, while escorts out on the port quarter began hoisting their attack flags, which indicated to everyone that submarines were closing now that the marauding aircraft were leaving. Steaming at full speed, still at Action Stations with all watertight doors and scuttles closed, as they had been all day, she cut across the lines of ships as she made for the danger zone, but under-estimated the speed and turning power of one of the old rust buckets that were giving Britain such sterling service.

With her upper deck swamped and holds heavily laden with provisions for our denuded shops, that merchant ship was no match for our sleek shape as we swept across her bows.

Both ships tried hard to turn aside as they closed, but the collision, when it came, ripped away the *Wellington's* side from the funnel to A gun. Luckily for us, the damage was all above the water line.

Such was the desperate need for ships at this time that I can still recall the aircraft that arrived next day to photograph the damage. And a week later when we got home, those darned Yanks, who had arrived in Londonderry while we had been away, had a new section built from those photographs, waiting to be fitted. Cranes hoisted it into position and welders and riveters worked throughout the night. By next day all that was required was for us to paint in the new camouflage.

In an attempt to improve relations, we were ordered to entertain a bus load of American sailors that would arrive that evening at seven o'clock. It got off on the wrong foot right from the word go. One of them fell off the gangway while coming aboard. Our gangway was nothing to write home about, but it was ours. It was small and light and we carried it with us wherever we went. We made it as safe as possible and we crossed it hundreds of times. We painted it and even put fancy knots on its guard-rails. None of us had ever managed to fall off it.

It was a bitterly cold night and the generator that supplied us with power for heat and light had to choose that evening to go on the blink. Trying to play darts wearing duffle coats was difficult enough, but when a hastily dried American wearing some of our clothes lectured us on how to rig a gangway he came near to being used as the dartboard.

Vickery, one of our Leading Seamen, overcome by the thick cigar smoke, switched on the ventilation fan and cold night air blasted through the trunking around the messdecks and out of the eyeballs . "Ah," said one of our guests, holding up his half frozen hands to the icy wind, "Warm air. Our ship has got this. The temperature is controlled by a thermostat over the door there, just like yours." He was pointing to Fred's cap hanging on a hammock hook. There was no warm air; HMS *Wellington* didn't provide such comforts.

Dagworth, shivering, reached up and touched the lagged pipe crossing the length of the mess taking steam to the winch up on our forecastle. "This is the beer pipe, if you'd only brought your glasses . . ."

Vic jumped in quickly. "Daggy! You can make the tea."

The evening was endless, but there were no fights. They all went home at nine o'clock. The visit was not a success and as far as I know, wasn't repeated on any other ship.

I had not managed to see Kate again. We had very little time ashore between trips and here we were, with steam up, ready to go once more with the paint on our repaired side hardly dry. It was a still day, with a fine drizzly rain as the engines began that familiar rumble that had come to be a part of our life. The visibility was closing in all the time as we left Londonderry behind, and within minutes all we would see were the buoys marking out the channel. We passed one and couldn't see the next, and just moments later she came to a shuddering stop with her screws churning up brown mud and water.

The *Wellington* had run aground on the side of that bend, the first one after leaving the wall. Nothing we could do would shift her. She was stuck fast. Luckily, it was only mud, and not rocks.

For a while we had hopes of an unexpected evening ashore, but those were soon dashed. There was a desperate need for ships like ours, and as soon as the fog lifted, a string of barges were sent out to us and everyone aboard worked through the night to unload everything we had. When full, they were taken back to the base under guard and empty ones sent back.

By morning, every depth charge, every shell, boxes of ammunition, provisions, supplies, boats and kit had been unloaded. Sweaty and tired, we waited for the tug. There was still water and oil and us if the tug failed; at high water, with the tug hauling and our screws thrashing and all of us as far aft as we could get, she slid off into deep water with a noise like a hundred children slurping hot milk.

We were too tired to even cheer. Now we had to do it all again to put it back. We were one day late leaving Londonderry and met our convoy in the North Channel as they headed outwards.

This time it was Bathurst in West Africa. It seemed to be as much of a shock to the locals as it was to us. As soon as we stepped ashore from our own boats we were surrounded by children, all fighting to hold our hands. It was fun at first, walking along past grinning natives with as many as six little ones hanging on to each hand, but it got awkward when you wanted to light a cigarette or wipe away the sweat.

But the children got tired of it too and left us alone after a while. There were some lovely houses on each side of the road and further along, an immaculate race-course. Then there was the church and a church hall, and in the hall the ladies from those lovely houses had set up tea and biscuits for their unexpected visitors. Heaven alone knows where they got that great big urn that took two of them to lift; it was hardly the thing from the vicarage garden. They were thin and looked drained by the heat, and all of them had that yellow colour from long use of Mepacrine. I think most of us began to understand some of the hardships that must have been suffered at those outposts of Empire, as they were called.

That was all of Bathurst. After wandering around in the afternoon heat for a while it was an early return to the ships. Next day no one was too keen to go ashore, so we put our one marksman (at least he had a badge of crossed rifles on his arm which was supposed to prove he was a marksman) up in the crows nest with a rifle and ammunition to watch out for sharks, cut our scrambling nets loose, called away the duty boat's crew to lay off the ship, and those of us who could swim, which was nearly everyone, jumped or dived over the side into the river.

It was here I had my first encounter with a jellyfish that had a sting in its tail. I swam into it. If our marksman had mistaken me for a shark and shot me in the chest it couldn't have felt worse. I could have made it back to the net under my own steam but the duty boat could see I was in trouble and came to my assistance. By the time we reached the ship my chest was red and swelling and it took nearly three days for that sting to disappear.

On our voyage home there were all kinds of rumours about overdue repairs. The *Wellington* badly needed dry docking, so it was welcome news when in the Irish Sea and passing the Isle of Man to be ordered to Dundee for refitting.

Refit! A month or more in safety ashore. Everyone was in high spirits as we turned away from the convoy with hoots of farewell and headed northwards again. It didn't matter that we had to spend another night at sea as we crashed our way around the north of Scotland, with the *Wellington* flinging back the cold water of the Minches over her forecastle and sent it dripping down the turret of A gun and across the front of her bridge. We were nearly home, home safe from the sea. With a new town to explore and new girls to meet. Home leave to come and a new and more dangerous ship would be ours to take back into the Atlantic to sprinkle those depth charges our Commander in Chief had been talking about in Londonderry.

But Dundee. Where was that? What was wrong with Liverpool

or Glasgow? We had girls in those places. Girls that had half promised things that young men would have travelled half the world for. But to us Dundee was spelt the same way as heaven. For four precious weeks or more, unavoidable interruptions to the war at sea offered youthful spirits the chance to be themselves.

"Hey, Jock. What's the girls like in Dundee?" And always the same answer from the Scots among us.

"Too bloody good for you lot!" We smiled to ourselves at the expected response as we brought HMS *Wellington* into the Scottish port of Dundee.

She was rusty and weather-beaten, and the weeds and shellfish that festooned her bottom would have kept a fish shop supplied for a month. The damage she had suffered by coming alongside burning ships at sea, and the storms that had buckled her plates and strained her engines must have been apparent to all of the welcoming committee on the dockside. This was no ordinary ship just coming in for repairs, but a real warship, limping in from that awful war zone of the North Atlantic, needing succour. Dundee had been favoured to receive her, and the repair yards of Dundee would restore her and send her back into the Western Approaches with a message from Scotland. 'This is from us.'

With two suitcases full of treasures from the North Atlantic and Africa, which H.M. Customs and Excise had failed to inspect at Dundee, I waited for mother to answer the bell at our front door in the Rhondda Valley.

Convinced it was the rent man, she was not eager to answer, and when at last she opened it and saw me it was a treasure to savour for ever.

With packets of dried bananas, Ju-Ju's and lucky charms from the markets of Africa, silk stockings and scents from Main Street in Gib, and some tins of corned beef snatched from empty lifeboats, tins of tobacco from the ships store, cigarettes and bars of soap, it was no wonder I was welcomed home almost as a conquering hero.

With tongue in cheek, mother mentioned that Susan was due home from Croydon at the weekend, and after giving me enough time to digest this, told me that a friend of hers, who had a caravan in nearby Porthcawl, a seaside resort, could easily be persuaded to lend me the key.

I glanced at mother, but she avoided my eyes. Susan was someone that she felt was special, someone she approved of. I valued her judgement too much to cast it aside with just a snap of the fingers.

"When you were young, mam, did you have someone that you would have gone to a caravan in Porthcawl with, and to hell with the consequences?"

She pulled me into those ample bosoms that once must have cuddled a first world war soldier, and as she kissed my forehead I could visualise those soldiers in khaki that had shaped her generation.

"How d'you think I got your dad?" she whispered, as she held me close.

I kissed her cheek as the moment passed. "I'll take that caravan," I told her with a grin, "but Sue will probably have other ideas. Your golden boy might not be what she wants".

As if from a long way off I heard her voice, "And who do you think it was who suggested the caravan?"

I pursed my lips in a silent whistle. This looked like being an exciting home leave. I looked at my mother with a new respect; she was my mother, just like a million other mothers; I counted myself lucky to have her.

I watched the train coming to the station bringing Sue home to me from Croydon. She stepped off onto the platform with a big suitcase and stood looking at me as the train pulled out again on its way to the next stop. A brown coat that reached to just below her knees, open at the neck, showed me her white sweater. She stood on the platform holding her suitcase, waiting for me to walk towards her.

If Tom had walked out of the waiting room at that moment I would have smashed him into the flower beds at the edge of the platform. She put her case down just as I reached her and her arms came around my neck as I held her tight. She was just as lovely as when I had seen her in Sheerness. I remembered how she looked when she walked away from me in that hospital ward and she had turned at the door and looked back at me.

I had been ill then, recovering from pneumonia. I wasn't ill now though, and there were stirrings that blotted out the appreciative stares of the Porters that watched from further along the platform.

I showed her the key for the caravan in Porthcawl. "Shall we catch the next train back to Porthcawl. Or is it Tom and mother?"

Without a word she handed me her suitcase and led me to the bridge across the rails for the train to Porthcawl.

It was nearly dark when we found our caravan. As we lit the gas lamps and made up the bed, I couldn't help but compare this lovely evening with my life at sea in HMS *Wellington*. After walking along the promenade and out to the pier, we made our way back through the moonlight to our caravan, and with a full moon shining on the water and sending shimmering flashes of silver like a pathway to the beach, my Susan undressed in our bedroom and stood there in front of me, holding out her arms.

I was finding it difficult to breathe again. She was bathed there in moonlight from the uncurtained window, and as my arms went around her and she pulled me close, I could feel those full and firm breasts that had tormented my night thoughts back there in Sheerness pressed against my chest. I shut my eyes as the sheets closed around us and as my lips closed on hers I felt her warm arms holding me close and the *Wellington*, Londonderry, Liverpool and Glasgow, were as nothing as we clung together in the moonlight. I went to sleep that night cradled in her arms and she held me to her breast as if I was a baby.

We spent a weekend there in Porthcawl that no one can ever spoil, and the card she had sent me for my twenty first birthday with 'They're Off!' on the front and the little knickers on the inside was propped on the shelf where we both could see it. On our last morning when I asked her to marry me, she kissed my cheek as we lay naked in each others arms.

"You go your way," she told me, "and I'll go mine. If you come safely home when this is all over and you still want me, you know where I live. I hope you'll ask me again then." I held her close and kissed her breasts. The thought of Tom enjoying these sent ripples of fire through my muscles. But it was her wish. If someone else could win her favours, I could hardly complain. We were living in dangerous times; it seemed to make sense to enjoy life when you could.

All too soon, leave was over and it was a long journey back by train through Crewe, Carlisle, Glasgow, Edinburgh and on to Dundee. We found our ship cold and unwelcoming, with engines and boilers stripped and our Heads roped off. Power was supplied by cable from ashore, but at least we still had the galley working to cook our meals and keep the tea brewing. The Duty Watch were reduced to just a skeleton crew; they had to stay aboard but everyone else escaped ashore and we made our meeting place in the Salvation Army Hostel nearby, almost taking the place over completely. The Superintendent went out of his way to make us feel at home and we bought our meals there and slept there, except for the nights when we were on duty and had to be aboard.

CHAPTER TWELVE

Bonnie Dundee quickly became home to us. After just one day exploring the town we were on first name terms with many of the girls and were soon enjoying a cuddle on the back seats of the cinema. One of the films we saw was *Pride and Prejudice*. I can remember the argument I had with Mary about how to pronounce prejudice. and while we were sorting it out in the foyer, Fred came down the stairs from the posh seats up in the balcony sounding like a tank, and the girl he was with lectured him on how to come down a flight of stairs with grace and dignity. Nonplused, he went back up and came down again, this time like a tank with a broken track.

We had a lot of fun later at sea, coming down ladders. He used to come down the ladder from the boat deck to the quarterdeck carrying an imaginary basket of flowers, hand on hips, struggling to keep his balance against the *Wellington's* attempts to throw him off, and Geordy watching from below with open mouth, then chasing him forward, opening his flies threateningly as he went.

That Superintendent of the Salvation Army Hostel did a magnificent job. He made sure that none of us managed to bring our girls into that establishment for any meals or for any other purpose. He never seemed to sleep or go off duty. Mind you, we did find other ways in apart from the front door, but someone wearing skirts would find some difficulty in getting in that way.

We developed several diversions, such as a fire in the kitchens, or a flood in the bathroom. Getting Agnes in through the toilet window to please Ginger took us ages. She was a big girl and got stuck half in and half out. Ginger was older than we were and perhaps should have known better, but then so was Agnes. I could see her yellow bloomers as I pushed from behind.

Mary was one of those normal good girls. If I as much as accidentally touched her hip she would glare at me and I would be ready to duck. Chopper, on the other hand, seemed to be living with Alison. He would disappear as soon as we came ashore. Sometimes we would see them together sitting in the cinema. She was a pretty girl, with big eyes, and he did his best to keep her well away from us. She seemed to like chocolate too. Anyone who didn't want their ration from our NAAFI, Chopper would buy it.

Then one night we cornered them and refused to let him pass. Reluctantly it seemed, he introduced us. Alison was divorced and had two little boys, so we knew where the chocolates were going. From then on everyone bought chocolates and passed them to Chopper.

One day when we were cleaning and oiling the Oerlikons, we saw Alison and her little boys on the wall alongside. We couldn't do much about Alison, but we took her two boys from her and they toured the ship. Up on the gun deck, Fred strapped one of them into the Oerlikon. We had already fitted a magazine to it before we saw them, and he cocked it and aimed it at a cross on the top of a church spire we could see over the roofs of the town. Unable to believe what he was contemplating, I snatched away the little boy's fingers from the trigger and snapped on the safety catch.

"Fred! Get off the gun deck!" For a moment I thought he had gone mad and was going to refuse. Then he laughed and unbuckled the little chap. That church had come within a whisker of requiring a new steeple.

One night after taking our girls home at a respectable time (I think Mary's father was waiting and watching from his bedroom window) we had stopped off on the way back for a few drinks of stronger beverage than we could get in our hostel and were wending our happy way home, closely followed by some local police who were making sure we got home safely.

Somehow we had collected a man of the cloth who was doing his best to hide his dog collar, and our Superintendent didn't know how to deal with him. There was no piano in the hostel but there was a piano accordion. Our sky pilot couldn't play that, so we compromised. Someone sat on the accordion, another pulled and pushed at one end, and the vicar played the other end as he would a piano. Never had the Salvation Army hostel seen such a night. The Superintendent danced a waltz with Ginger, which had all of us passing uneasy glances at each other, while Agnes struggled angrily to get out of the toilet window.

Gradually, they were putting the *Wellington* back together again. She looked different, but no more so than she did after almost every spell in harbour as new equipment was added. This time she had radar, and along with her direction finders, radio aerials and new paintwork, she seemed a lot different to the battle scarred old warrior we had brought in here.

Our time in Dundee was coming to an end. We knew it, and so of course did the dockyard workmen who were preparing her. One evening as I strolled through the park with my arm around Mary, she pulled me off the path into the trees. We stood hidden from the road, leaning against a tree. There was just a hint of tears in her eyes.

"You'll be leaving Scotland soon," she said. "Will you miss me?

I rubbed my nose against hers as my arms slid around her waist. I had enjoyed her company; it had been innocent enough. We had laughed, had fun. Quarrelled once or twice. In another kind of life I would soon have acquired a Scottish accent, and seen her take our children to Sunday school. I kissed her there in the shelter of the trees. She would make some lucky man a home and bless him with children that he would be proud of. In a saner world, it could so easily have been me. For a while we clung together, remembering those good times. Then, with our arms round each other we walked back to the path and to reality.

The clang of the engine room telegraphs signalled the start of that familiar rumble that spread throughout the length of the ship as her engines came alive. All through the previous day we had loaded and distributed ammunition, and depth charges had been secured in every available place along the quarterdeck. Ready use lockers were full, and 4.7 inch shells were in their holders around each of the guns.

There had been no shore leave on that last day as we got HMS *Wellington* ready for sea. All our tearful goodbyes had been said, and all through the night power and steam had been increasing ready for this moment. Hoses had washed away the dirt of the dockyard, cranes had lifted out welding sets, lines of supply trucks had been unloaded, a new ensign had been hoisted, and was fluttering gently in the breeze, heat was shimmering above the funnel and steam escaping slowly from her siren.

All along the walls of the dock the men who had worked on her were gathering with their families to watch her leave. They had done their part, and had returned her to us. Now it was our turn.

The *Wellington* eased away from the wall, screws churning the water into white froth. Her disciplined crew, all smartly dressed in uniform, stood motionless. It seemed as if all the girls we knew were there, calling; many were crying, blowing kisses, waving handkerchiefs. We watched silently, motionless, unable even to wave. I saw Mary standing with an older man, probably her father. I saw her point as she saw me and she waved. He lifted his hand, but I just had to stand there in silent regret; I couldn't wave back.

There was Alison and her two little sons, both of them were calling to Chopper. Out of the corner of my eye I saw him shut his eyes so as not to see; he couldn't shout back. Standing alone, and not waving, was Agnes.

From the siren on the funnel above, the *Wellington* blasted a farewell to bonnie Dundee that must have been heard over all of the town. At least, they hadn't altered the penetrating power of that. The figures on the wall became smaller and indistinct as we sailed away, but still we watched, until they could no longer see us, and as HMS *Wellington* began lifting to the swell of the open ocean we broke ranks as the safety of the land faded behind.

Soon, the dirt and the grease and the excesses of the land began churning our stomachs, and one by one, men began disappearing in the direction of the Heads. Once it was up, you were back to normal again, almost as clean as the wind that blew about her upperworks and along her decks taking the last speck of dust away with it.

With no welcoming lights from the land to guide her or speed her on her way, she headed into the darkness with the hissing sea caressing her sides and the whine of the turbines thrusting her onwards. How quickly we put the comforts and safety of home behind us, as wrapped against the cold night wind we clutched our binoculars and studied the dark horizon. There was no barbed wire or trenches out here, but it was a no man's land just the same, a hostile place where every flicker of light was an enemy or a danger. No one ever struck a match on the open upper deck or drew on an unguarded cigarette.

Occasionally we would feel the deck pressing under our feet as she lifted over a bigger than usual swell, then they would fall away from under us as she went down the other side. The hissing would grow louder as she sank deeper and the water rose higher along her sides. At moments like that we would turn our backs to the way she was travelling, as she could nastily dip her bows right under and toss a ton or more of cold sea water into the air for the wind to spray back over half her length.

If she was being pushed forward fast enough in bad weather she could drop over a big wave quickly enough to leave her propellers out of the water, and the whine of the turbines would rise to a scream as her screws free wheeled. Then she would shudder as if laughing as they bit into the sea again. That shudder would shake any tea or sugar out of every unfastened locker. The shouts of rage coming from the men off watch below could be heard by the Duty Watch up on the black and waterswept deck as they guided her safely onwards.

After supper, someone from below would bring up fannies of scalding tea and a handful of cups, and while those below were washing the dishes, hot cups of tea would be passing up to the bridge and wheelhouse and to the gun turrets. Supper for the watch on deck would be kept hot in the galley, and they in turn would pass up tea and cups to the watch on deck as they washed up and put away their dishes. By nine o'clock, hammocks would be slung and men were turning in. Lights would be switched off as someone finished reading, and soon only the police lights would be left and the hammocks would swing with the motion of the ship. All hammocks were hauled right up almost flat; you could always walk about on the mess decks under the hammocks. The sound of the sea rushing along her side was always present, and to most of us it was a lullaby as familiar as home. Let it stop and instantly everyone was awake, tense, and waiting.

After testing all systems in the Moray Firth, the *Wellington* rounded Duncansby Head into the Pentland Firth on a fine sunny morning that was doing its best to compensate after losing our friends back in Dundee. Most of us had recovered our sea legs after a lively night and had started to eat again. The *Wellington* was cracking on speed to rendezvous with an outward bound convoy South of Ireland, and everyone was busy clearing up after so long in harbour. There seemed so much to do, the seaboats were moving as the new gripes stretched. One of the carley floats had almost washed off during the night, guard-rails needed tightening all along each side.

We caught up with the convoy the following morning and, after parading our new shape and paintwork to the other escorts, took up our usual position zig-zagging in the lead, bound this time for Lagos, close to the equator in Nigeria.

Just as darkness stole over the sea our direction finders began picking up signals showing that this convoy had been found by unwelcome marauders. Shaded blue signal lights, aimed through tubes, so that they could only be seen by those they were aimed at, blinked a warning to other ships. Action Station bells caught everyone on the hop once more, just as they always did, only this time, more so after so long in harbour.

"Where did we put our anti-flash gear?" "Anybody seen my lifebelt?" "Here, put one of these on." Urgent, whispered words passing around. Chalky was worried; he had left a kettle of hot water on the mess table after washing the supper dishes. He hadn't had time to empty it; it was still there. We all knew what would happen to it. She would be speeding up soon, and if she turned then that kettle would slide off the table into someone's locker. We all hoped she would turn in the other direction, so it would slide off harmlessly onto the messdeck. It didn't stop us calling Chalky all sorts of names for putting us into such danger; he should have had the sense to put the thing on the deck where it couldn't have done much harm.

Suddenly our new radar picked up a blip ahead and within seconds, the forward 4.7 smashed off three star shells, the gun flashes lighting up the whole ship. Moments later there were three reddish yellow bursts in the sky a long way ahead of us, rapidly changing the dark sea into bright moonlight as the flares blossomed and swung on their parachutes, and there in the man made pathway of silvery light was a black shape striving to submerge.

Captain of A gun was Vickery, and Shorty Bates, our diver, was the gun layer, but there were seven of them in the team altogether and they got off two shots which were near misses before the submarine went under.

Coloured flares from the Commodore's ship while this was going on was turning the convoy out of the way. With the

Wellington increasing quickly to full speed ahead, orders were flashing for the depth settings as the Oerlikon crews raced for the quarterdeck.

Three hundred feet! Stand by. Without slackening speed or turning we could hear the rattle as the charge from the rails released, but the noise of the wind and the thunder of the propellers and rushing of the wake just underneath us drowned the splash as it hit the water.

With the depth keys in our hands we waited for the bells, ready to pull the firing pin.

Now! Bang! Blinded by the flash and burnt by the flame we must reload. The next thrower fires while we are half way through, and the rattle of the charges rolling out of the rails over the stern urges us on.

There isn't time to watch the chaos in the sea behind us, but when there is the detonation can be seen deep in the ocean like a huge white sheet being briefly waved, and the spouts of water shoot up like a monster from the deep leaping out with open arms much higher than the mast of our ship.

"Depth setting five hundred feet. Stand by!"

Ready again. "Where the hell did they put our flash gear? My face is burning."

"Piss on it, that's supposed to be good."

Hang on, she's turning again, heeling over at speed, the quarterdeck almost in the water as she pushes around. Not much hope for that kettle of water now. Hope it wasn't my locker it went into! There goes the rails, our turn any second now. Then the firing bell. Pull! Jesus! That burnt.

From off to our left there was a white flash that seemed to linger in the dark, unwilling to go out. One of the ships of the convoy was dying out there. So there was more than one submarine after this convoy. One thing was for sure; the one fighting for its life under us was no danger to them. Sprinkle them like salt, our C in C had told us. And that is exactly what we were doing. Eight charges to a pattern, and we laid pattern after pattern over that wily submarine.

There was no soot from our newly swept galley chimney or engine room funnel, and the cables and rivets, plates and stays from Dundee held fast and secure. But furniture, light fittings, dishes, tea, sugar, flour, had gone the way they always went after a prolonged attack.

Sometime during the night a watertight hatch opened and a fanny of tea and some cups were passed up from below. The attack had slackened and it looked like we were losing our quarry, but we all had the feeling that she wasn't going to be of much danger to anybody from now on. We could hear and feel other depth charges being fired from a long way off; they felt, and sounded like, sledge-hammer blows on the ships side below the water line.

We had lost contact, and after searching for several hours abandoned the hunt and went after the convoy. Two ships had been lost during the night; the survivors were aboard other ships and no one had been left adrift. Back on course, we were bound once more for Lagos.

The kettle of washing up water had ended up in Chalky's locker. A fitting punishment, we thought, for such carelessness. Our anti-flash gear had been found in the cork lifebelt locker abaft the funnel and was now safely stowed in the ready use ammunition boxes. Someone in Dundee had walked off with a few of our steel helmets but these had now been replaced. We were battle scarred professionals again after being allowed to get soft in Dundee.

With warmer weather as we progressed Southwards, white shirts and shorts became the rig of the day. Buckets of underclothes and white uniforms soaking in soap flakes littered the bathroom floor, and one evening we could hear Geordy singing lustily as he showered.

"Take a pair of Sparkers eyes.

And a pair of Buntings hips."

He could be heard throughout the ship and his voice ended in a shriek as an irate sparker (telegraphist) threw a bucket of cold water over him. But then half the ship's company would take up the refrain, much to the chagrin of the Signalman's mess.

At times the sea could be as smooth as glass. So smooth that you could see a fish jumping a long way off, and the splash would draw every pair of binoculars as quickly as if it had been a scream for help. There was always a swell on the ocean, which made it unsafe to open any of the messdeck portholes. The *Wellington* would glide smoothly along at the head of her convoy with the glassy sea hissing gently along her sides. Then some misguided nit would open the portholes and stick his head out to fill his lungs with pure air. If we had been scrubbing decks with the hosepipes filling the scuppers with seawater about then, any overflow would drop down straight into the open port hole. If it was later in the day when scrubbing decks was finished, then one of those unpredictable swells would lift the sea up her sides, and any open portholes would draw bursts of wet sea water into the messdecks. It was no wonder that the brass butterfly nuts on the portholes and deadlights were more than finger tight, and the drip tins under each of them were emptied every morning.

The morning watch, from 0400 to 0800, was the one that gave us time to have breakfast. The Bosuns Mate, who knew the position of all of our hammocks, as we all did, would shake us at 0345, and we would come awake from our personal dream of being wrapped in the arms of the girl we loved to see his unshaven face staring up at us. There would just be time to get dressed and collect a cup of cae before climbing out onto the upper deck and taking over the watch.

Supper had been at six o'clock the night before, which was a long time ago. Just after dawn, once that early danger time had been passed, we would leave our guns and search along the scuppers for any stranded flying fish. They would never fly in onto the low quarterdeck; it was always the forecastle scuppers where we would find them, as many as six or ten in a night, where they lifted out of the water to get away from the *Wellington's* hissing bows.

We would see them during the day as well, rising in shoals from the sea in front of us, but they always flew away from us then, but at night, many of them would end up in the scuppers along our forecastle. At 0800 on being relieved, we would hungrily take our fish off to the mess to prepare them for breakfast, trying to remember how our mothers dealt with them. If any of them had moved, we would have screamed and threw them back.

At that time in the morning, with one watch up on deck and the other working part of ship, we would have the galley to ourselves and could cook them in any way we could remember. To hungry young men they tasted just like trout.

The routine of Up Spirits at eleven o'clock was a regular and welcome event, and was carried out in the same way and in the same place always, and Chef, our Petty Officer cook, was always there in his galley cooking the dinner while the rum was being measured and distributed outside his galley window, and always he would watch and lick his lips as any surplus was emptied into the galley sink.

Then one awful Saturday morning the gash running party forgot about a bucket of washing up water and with the Inspecting Officers fast approaching, there was nothing for it but to hide it temporarily in the diving store.

The cooks of the mess held their breath as our Captain inspected the gleaming cutlery laid out in a fan formation on the table, ran his finger over some pipes overhead, cast his eyes over the white table and well scrubbed cork lino. Satisfied, he moved on to the next mess and everyone breathed again. All they had to do now was get rid of that bucket of dirty water while he was inspecting somewhere else before he got to the diving store.

Dagworth had that task, and as soon as our Captain was out of sight he dashed off with it to the nearest sink, the one in the galley. He got there just after the surplus rum had been emptied through the window from the passage, and as his greasy dishwater sloshed into the sink, Chef's scream of agony brought the Captain, our Jaunty, the Duty Officer and everybody in the passage to the galley to see what had happened.

Leading Seaman Scargill was holding Chef, while Dagworth was fleeing for his life.

"Dirty water in the clean, white sink," explained Scargill lamely.

While Dagworth complained. " 'e had a bloody great knife in his hand!"

From then on, Scargill was as happy as Chef was after tot time. And we eyed the little curtain beneath the galley sink with a knowing humour.

Lagos was a much larger place than Freetown, but at that time in its development we still had to anchor, swing out the lower boom, lower our seaboats, and rig our best gangway from the low quarterdeck. Once ashore we found we could hire cycles and ride off for the day with our bathing suits to out of town beaches. There were open air cinemas, which was like being in someone's garden facing a white wall, and any film that had a black face amongst the actors, like Jack Benny's Rochester, would receive roars of excited applause from the mainly black audience.

It would be only twilight when we watched any of those films, as we were expected back aboard before it got really dark. The markets were always fascinating with their strange smells and fruits. The big hands of bananas on sale at every stall always drew crowds of us. They were so available here, but impossible to obtain back at home. We used to carry back to our ship arms full of big bananas they called plantains, and then wondered why we weren't hungry for supper.

Because of problems with her asdics, the *Wellington* had to make use of a floating dry dock in Lagos, and being high and dry, with no toilets, no water, no power, we couldn't live aboard. For a few days we had to be accommodated ashore, and by the time we got back aboard again, all manner of things had happened to us.

It was there in Lagos that I sat my examination for Leading Seaman. I scratched like mad in the heat of the examination room as I wrestled with the questions on the examination papers. Safely back on board the *Wellington* once more and out of that hated dry dock, we eyed each other suspiciously as we scratched away. It was no surprise when the Bosun's Mate piped a short arm inspection for that afternoon.

Everyone on the ship would have to go through this. It was no use most of us being sweet and pure if someone escaped the inspection to infect us all again. In a long line we wound our way through the sick bay where our doctor was ticking names off a long list and poor Doc was sitting on a low stool peering through his thick spectacles and using a magnifying glass as big as his head.

This was Lagos, close to the Equator. It was stinking hot, so all we had on was shorts. We were expected to stand in front of Doc and drop them, while he closely examined our prized possessions through his magnifying glass, looking for those tiny crab-like things that were causing all the scratching.

With Geordy acting the goat in front of me, and Fred trying to stroke from behind, I was in no fit state to be inspected when I dropped my shorts in front of poor Doc. It must have looked like an about to be erected telegraph pole through that magnifying glass he was using. It was no wonder he fell off his stool. There was no hesitation in his command however.

"Shave off!"

I like to think that was a comment of admiration at what I was revealing. Nevertheless, I joined the rest in the bathroom shaving the hair off and using that blue unction stuff so beloved by the Navy. No one believed us when we swore we caught them from the lavatory seats while we were in dry dock.

"Only Parsons catch these things from lavatories," lectured our doctor, scratching quietly. "You lot have been up to something."

Doc promised us faithfully that the doctor would shave off as well, and he, personally, would inspect him." You are not to worry", he told us. "You are all pure and virginal and I shall make sure you all stay that way."

We looked at him suspiciously, not sure how to take that remark.

Oblivious to what was happening in the Western Approaches, now in the most dangerous period of the war, we were young men chasing the girls, no matter what colour they were. As Geordy said, "I started off getting stuck into a pillow. She was black, the room was black; when she switched off the light I couldn't bloody find her."

We stared in disbelief at the biggest bunch of bananas we had ever seen. It was the size of one of our trees back home After a violent argument, Fred bought it for two pounds; a phenomenal amount in those days. It was too heavy for us to carry, so we persuaded one of our Navy trucks to get it back to the embarkation point. The Coxswain of our liberty boat had to be threatened before he agreed to taking it aboard, and the Duty Officer walked round it a few times after we had struggled up onto the quarterdeck with it.

This was the same boat that brought off one of our sparkers who had acquired a monkey. It was being mistreated in the market by its owner who had been swinging it around on the end of a rope, and a near riot had developed as we chased him among the stalls. A few packets of cigarettes gathered from all of us, and we had a new pet to go with the cat that had joined us by mistake in Dundee.

We took HMS *Wellington* out of Lagos with a monkey in the rigging and the biggest bunch of green bananas you ever saw hanging in the diving store. The cat stalked that monkey but couldn't climb the rigging, and the monkey waited until the cat wasn't watching, then jumped on her. We provided them with a cardboard box on the upper deck with a door cut in it and the cat took refuge inside, while the monkey sat on top of the box waiting for the cat to stick its head out, then, thump!

Those two creatures provided us with hours of fun as they fought around that box. Of all the people aboard for the monkey to take a dislike to it had to be our Captain. Whenever he appeared, we would stand aside at attention, waiting for him to pass. If we were coming up a ladder, and he showed up at the top, we would promptly slide back down again and respectfully give him the right of way.

But the monkey was a different proposition. If it was sitting on the hand rail of a ladder and the Captain appeared, they would stare at each other. The monkey would gibber with bared teeth and our Captain would stand back glaring, waiting for the monkey to get out of the way. Several times we saw him abandon his journey and go back to his cabin rather than pass that monkey.

Far out to the westwards the convoy turned, and with the North Star bright in the sky ahead of us and the ring around the moon getting smaller as the barometer dropped, we noted with rising concern the pressure lowering hour by hour as the mighty Atlantic seemed to be closing its ranks on the tiny dots that strove to cross it. Fingers of high cirrus cloud began stealing across the moon as the swell increased and by nightfall the decks were wet with spray being thrown back from her plunging bows.

Duffle coats had to give way to seaboots and oilskins, and well turned down sou'westers took the place of balaclavas as the sea began coming inboard. Supper was an unpleasant affair with the galley unable to cope with the unexpected violent motion. Hatches and ventilators were closed off as the sea lashed the upper deck. People began turning in early, weary of trying to keep their balance as the *Wellington* plunged along her course.

By 0800 when the new watch on deck took over, the night was

fearsome. The low quarterdeck was a mass of swirling white water that would have been suicide for anyone to venture on. 'A' gun's crew had been withdrawn to the wheelhouse, nothing could have survived forward of the bridge. The lookouts on the bridge itself clung to the steel wings as they peered out at a world gone mad, and in the blackness of the night, the *Wellington* shook almost continuously as her screws came out of the water and her steering engine strove to keep her on course.

When the middle watch took over at midnight a new and more fearsome war had been declared. Nature was in command now, and all we could do was pray.

Depth charges began tearing loose from their lashings along the waist and were soon rolling along the sea washed deck. Sailors with heaving lines tied around their waists were sent after them, and pushed them overboard with their feet. As she altered course at the end of a zig-zag she went over so far that for one awful moment all on deck, hanging on to something solid, feared she wasn't going to come back. From below we could hear crashes as furniture toppled, and we saw the starboard seaboat reaching the water and tearing away from its gripes. One of the falls carried away, and the boat was left hanging there, its bows touching the water on every roll and swinging violently back as the sea hit it.

There was nothing for it but to cut it free as it battered at the ships side, and we watched it swirl away into the night. All attempts at zig-zagging or even of escorting now had to be abandoned. It was a fight for life and nothing else. The *Wellington* turned away from the awful wind and sea, and ran with it.

An angry red dawn began spreading over an empty sea. Giant sized waves seemed to be escorting us along. Sometimes they would overtake us, and topple over onto the quarterdeck, and boiling white water would surge over everything, right up to the turret of 'B' gun. The steering engine would shake the ship like a terrier with a rag as it strove to keep her stern from being pushed around so that the marching sea could overwhelm us.

Increasing speed to avoid the high waterfalls trying to descend on her stern had to be balanced with the valleys that were opening out in front of her. She had to keep going forward faster than the foaming waves coming up from behind, or they would have pushed her broadside to and capsized her. Her bows seemed to come out of a mountain top with a valley spread out below her. They would topple over, leaving her screws clear of the water, shaking the ship, then she would run down the hillside like a bus out of control. We would feel the speed building up as she rushed down hill towards the valley bottom, with a mass of white flecked water as high as the Post Office Tower barring her progress like a wall.

Wrapping our arms around anything solid, we would hold our breath as she rushed headlong down the hillside, and the wall of water in front of us grew rapidly higher until it towered above us.

But it couldn't swamp us. All watertight doors and scuttles had long since been closed off. Only the watch on deck was vulnerable, and they well knew her tricks. They had the task of keeping her safe, and only moved when her corkscrewing and plunging motion gave them chance to shift from handhold to handhold.

As she raced down hill into what looked like a solid wall of water, everyone who had to be abroad on the upper deck made sure he was abaft the bridge and holding onto something that couldn't carry away. Like a butcher's cleaver she would knife into the watery obstruction, and it felt as if the driver was standing on the brakes. The wall would collapse in a roar of rushing water smashing down on her fore parts and foaming along each side of her gun decks. She would force upwards like a cork, water pouring off her. Then she would do it all again.

The flash screen that projected forward from the Captain's cabin to protect those of the hedgehogs deck from the burning flash of 'A' gun, was forced upwards by one of these walls of water bursting inboard, and not long after, the barrel of 'A' gun was smashed up in the same way. All through a long and dangerous day we kept her running with the storm, trying to repair damage as it occurred.

Supper that night for Number Two mess was sausages and mash. I held a large dish of about forty fried sausages and bravely made my way from the galley towards the Seaman's mess forward, across the open space of the Stoker's mess, with nothing to hold on to, and no hands spare even if there was. Feeling her lifting as she climbed one of those mountain peaks, I spread my legs in panic as I prepared for what was coming next. The corkasine was firm under my feet as she lifted, then she went over the top and started to drop, and I was as light as a feather as the deck fell from under me. I crashed into the wall of the sick bay with an injured shoulder and a cut knee, but with forty sausages still intact.

Among many cheers, and before I could move, the bitch went up and over once more, and me and those sausages were spread all over the Stoker's messdeck.

Corned beef sandwiches were all we could manage for day after day. On the third day our prized potato locker broke adrift. It was nearly full, and was very heavy. It slid across the deck into the guard rails. As the *Wellington* slipped over the top of one of those awesome peaks, it slid forward, wiping stanchion after stanchion away. As she reached the bottom and tilted to climb, back it came, wiping away all the guard rails, until it crashed into our motorboat. We couldn't save it, or any of the spuds inside it. Over it had to go, along with the remains of the motorboat.

Every day, Fred and me inspected the hundreds of bananas hanging in the diving store that was supposed to remind our families back home of the fruit that had vanished from wartime Britain. And every day we noted with dismay the wet blackness that was spreading over them, and the pungent smell that was seeping out over the messdeck. At last we reluctantly gave in, and agreed that our well meant investment had been a mistake. We struggled up to the upper deck with them and dropped them overboard. It didn't help in the least as we saw the Lookouts gravely take off their hats as we consigned them to the deep.

For a couple of hair-raising hours our steering engine packed up through overwork, bearing out the Chief Engineer's dire warnings of what would happen if we turned the steering wheel too fast. But there was no help for it, we had to as we strove to prevent her turning, keeping her moving in step between the regiments of mountains marching along with us.

Men from the watch below had to be called out to man the steering wheel in the tiller flat back aft. Telephones were hurriedly rigged to pass the orders from the bridge to those who were now doing the steering, while all available engineers worked on repairing the steering engine. They had it working again before dark, and soon the reassuring shudder could be felt, and our Chief Engineer banged his head in anger as he felt his beloved engine protesting once more.

With no guard rails along most of the boat deck, it was now highly dangerous to be out on the upper deck at all. We did the best we could by rigging lines for people to hang onto as they moved from place to place.

With the upper deck constantly under water, and the noise of rushing seas drowning out all other sounds, men found some relief in the safety of their hammocks with a book. As the ship rolled, so would the hammocks swing, neutralising the effect. Only the up and down motion would you feel, as warm, dry, and snug on your pillow under your blanket, you watched the ceiling, or deck head as I should call it, close to your face, tilt from side to side. Sometimes you would tilt so far you almost touched it with your arm, then you would hear things that hadn't been fastened or secured go sliding along the deck below you, and you wondered if it was your seaboots, or your tin of ticklers, that had gone. By half-past eight, weary after a long day of combating nature and being still in the lead, you would put your book about *No Orchards for Miss Blandish*, with the corner of the page you were reading turned down, under your pillow, and try to sleep, listening to the storm pounding the deck just above your head, and smashing into her steel sides only feet away from where your hammock swung.

Your mates were up there, pushing the *Wellington* safely onwards. Guns were manned. Asdics were listening, Lookouts were watching, giros being followed. You felt that at last it was safe to put your arms around your Susan's or your Katy's, or your Mary's waist. Her shy protests as you slipped the straps of her nightdress down over her shoulders to reveal her breasts, and as your lips closed over her nipples her shuddering gasp forced your eyes open to see the unfortunate Bosun's Mate staring up at you as he shook your hammock.

"It's a quarter to twelve," he tells you, oblivious of what he has interrupted, and you glare down at him, ready to bite off his nose. The noise of the sea smashing on the deck above, and the sound of the water rushing past her sides drowns out any words spoken on the darkened mess deck.

Dressed ready for the weather in seaboots and oilskins, holding a cup of hot cocoa, I climbed out onto the upper deck from the midship hatch, and stared at a black world with specks of white that seemed to tower above me. A finger of green, like a pencil writing graffiti, raked across the sky as St Elmo's Fire lit up the mast and aerials. As my eyes got used to the darkness I saw the phosphorescent crests of the waves flickering all about us like a thousand camp fires burning on an empty plain. Fish could be seen swimming, leaving a trail of green fire behind them. A burst of storm water, flung up from the *Wellington's* bows, sprayed aft, draping phosphorescent jelly over upperworks and oilskins. My cup of cocoa had a green top which I decided to keep until morning to show to the others, but by daylight, it looked like a cold cup of cocoa, and as the cup was wanted, was emptied away. The green slime on my oilskins gave enough light to read the time from a watch, and scooped up with your hand and sloshed on a depth charge, it gave enough light to set a depth setting without a torch.

The Quarterdeck HMS Wellington.

The were green flashes all around us in that stormy night as we struggled to keep HMS *Wellington* running with the wind. Before dawn, two of the funnel stays had parted, and her funnel had tilted over, allowing smoke to come from her deck level. Later that day, for the first and only time I ever heard it, the Bosun's Mate came round piping a warning that the ship would make an alteration of course at 1300.

We had lost our convoy over a week ago, it had been every man for himself since then. Now, too far to the northwards, we would have to turn around and head back into the storm. But turning across the awful wind that was blowing would he highly dangerous.

CHAPTER THIRTEEN

At 1300, with everything secured, nothing on the galley stove, and all dishes washed and put safely away, and with the Captain on the bridge, it was 270 revolutions, and starboard twenty. The sea was a storm lashed wasteland with visibility almost zero as mountains, valleys, and peaks reached out to receive us. The *Wellington* lurched and heeled as she began her turn. Everyone, whether on or off watch, stopped to hang on to something firm as he waited for her to come around. As the wind and sea began to hit her she went over away from it, reeling like someone being beaten. Further and further over she listed as she came broadside to the wind and sea.

Everyone aboard was now holding their breath as she struggled to come around into the wind. At times, to us on the upper deck who were forcing her round, it seemed her yard arm was almost touching the water. Hard A'starboard. Full ahead! Get round, come on girl, you can do it! Hold on. And like a tired racehorse, with turbines screaming, and her steering engine shaking all on board as if she was angry with us, she came back into the storm and struggled upright, bows awash, tossing seawater aft, scuppers streaming.

Lips pursed in relief, it was half ahead, 150 revolutions, slow her down, steady girl, just breast it.

For another two long days we hung on there as the storm shrieked past us, then at last, as the awful weather began relenting, we risked turning for the safety of home. On the second day, a big freighter showed up ahead of us going the same way. Her upper deck cargo of large balks of timber had broken loose, and were hanging over her sides like a monstrous net as she struggled along.

We closed her slowly, looking at her buckled sides being hammered by the timber, and as we came within hailing distance, asked her if she needed any assistance.

We saw them eyeing us carefully through their binoculars, then, "Thank you, no. You look in more need of assistance than I do. Can I help you?"

We waved our thanks, and pulled slowly ahead. That was the only ship we saw out of a convoy of sixty that we had started off with. The boom defence vessels opened up for us to enter Loch Foyle, and watched us silently slide past without the usual protesting toot as we rocked them with our wake. Even the bum boats from Moville, laden with eggs and butter, shied away from us as if they expected us to sink at any moment.

Londonderry seemed more beautiful to us than it had ever looked as we stepped ashore. It took ages to get used to the floor being firm and steady. Whenever you stopped to talk to someone the pavement felt as if it was tilting, and you caught yourself walking with legs apart as once you did as a child with the insides of your legs spreathing.

Picking up some shaving soap from Woolworths, I handed the girl some money, and holding a ten shilling note between my fingers, stared at Katy on the other side of the counter. Her eyes opened wide as she saw me. She held one end of my ten bob note, and I held the other, and it tore gently across the middle as if I didn't want to let it go. She came round to my side of the counter. As if there was nobody else in the store, her arms went around my neck as she kissed me.

"You're eight days late," she told me at last as she held me at arms length, and in answer to my puzzled look. "According to my diary, you should have been here over a week ago. I thought you had been sent to Belfast again."

I laughed at her, wishing that all the lights would fail and the store would be plunged into darkness. Retreaving her half of my ten shilling note, I paid for my soap as she got back behind her counter. "What time do you finish?" I asked, as she passed over my change. Her white teeth were shining in the lights, and her lips were red and inviting as she looked at me.

"Six," she whispered, as she turned to serve another customer. "But I'll see you on the bridge at eight."

I nodded, "You bet!" I would have liked to wait for her right there, but I was getting in the way of too many people, I just waved and left.

We met on the bridge crossing the Foyle. Early November, 1943. It was a cold night, and very dark. HMS *Wellington* had just brought us safely home through a mighty storm. The cold wind coming off the river whipped over the bridge, and we turned the collars of our coats up as we hurried across. I cannot recall the film we saw, it was enough to get in out of the cold, find our seats, and cling together in the darkness. I was aware of her eyes filling with tears and reflecting the light of the screen at some part of the picture, and comparing this lovely moment with being awoken by the Bosun's Mate during the night watches. But this was no dream. This was real.

Katy turned her head to look at me as my arm tightened around her, unaware of what I had been doing to her in my dreams. We could not know we would never meet again. The war in the Atlantic had reached its peak, and the *Wellington* would not be allowed to stay out of it for long. Even now her next convoy would be assembling somewhere, but for tonight, this was enough. I had a girl in my arms, and I would keep her there all night if she would stay. I saw her white teeth as she smiled at me, then she kissed my cheek before turning back to look at the picture.

It was all over much too soon, and we were walking back over the windswept bridge, but now there was a half moon in the sky hiding briefly behind white clouds that passed across like schooners under full sail, and the same stars that had winked at us far out in the dangerous ocean now gleamed over Londonderry like lights shining through holes in black paper.

Again it was to the wall at the end of the street that she was taking me, but I was doing the navigating this time, and we stopped where we couldn't be seen, and just as if we both felt this was the last time, we clung together. I had my arms inside her warm coat, and her arms were inside my burberry. Then softly at first, we could hear the sound of engines in the sky, getting louder all the time until the pulsating drone seemed to be directly overhead. Pressed hard against the wall, we waited, holding fast to each other. But the bombs never came. Instead, the noise of the engines began to fade as they moved away. For a brief while our mad world seemed to have relented, and gave time for two lovers to kiss in the dark. I felt her warm cheek against mine, and my arms around her held her close. Her eyes in the moonlight were shining, just as they had been in the cinema.

Footsteps approaching us from the direction of the bridge ended a moment that would last a lifetime.

"Tomorrow?" Her voice was just a whisper.

I shook my head. Tomorrow would be the turn of the port watch ashore.

"The day after." Then I qualified it in case we had been sent to sea by then. "See you in Woolworths in the afternoon." I kissed her hand, and as if she knew this was goodbye, she pressed my hand against her cheek, then walked away out of my life.

Repairs had gone on almost from the moment the *Wellington* had come alongside. Within forty-eight hours she was ready for sea, and one of the last things they swung aboard and welded down was a new spud locker.

Almost on sailing time, a truck full of provisions arrived alongside, and there were only a few sacks of potatoes among them. Our new spud locker was less than half full as we set sail from Londonderry early on the morning that I would have been seeing Katy.

With five Escorts steaming in line ahead we negotiated the lovely river Foyle, and after leaving the loch turned right, passing through the North Channel and into the Irish Sea, and close to the Point of Ayre on the north tip of the Isle of Man to meet up with our convoy in Liverpool Bay. Taking them south of Ireland it was then straight out into the Atlantic Ocean with a strong air escort that we watched through our gun sights as they zoomed across us. Our lips tightened as they waggled their wings in farewell at eventide. They would be home in time for supper in the mess, their duty done. The unlucky ones would put down for an early call, so that perhaps they could be with us again tomorrow morning.

We blew up our lifebelts and studied the darkening horizon as our convoy plodded onwards, and dead on cue the port escort hoisted her attack flag and warned us all about it with a couple of blasts on her siren.

Coloured rockets fired immediately from the Commodore's ship turned the whole convoy ninety degrees to the right, away from the reported danger area, and the *Wellington* went to full ahead as Action Stations sounded throughout the ship.

Before she could reach full speed the Asdics were pinging on something to our left, and she heeled over as she turned to face the new danger with the sea coming inboard onto her low quarterdeck as the black flag was being hoisted aloft from her signal deck.

From the escort that was now ahead of the convoy we could hear her siren warning everyone that she had made contact as well, even though by now it was too dark to see her attack flag being hoisted.

Jesus Christ! They were all around us.

"Depth settings two hundred feet. Full ahead both. Fire!" More coloured rockets from the Commodore was turning the convoy back the way it had come as our depth charges began exploding in the speeding wake.

"Hard A'port. Five hundred feet. Steady as she goes. Fire! And without slackening speed the second pattern was spread over the target area.

No matter how fast she was travelling or turning, or how rapidly she demanded we fire, we were the experts. Years of practise, skill, resolve. Call it what you will, but HMS *Wellington* was a deadly weapon at this game, a sword with a finely honed edge, vastly different from the ship that went to sea with that first convoy from Plymouth.

Throughout the night, three warships waged their own private battle, sprinkling depth charges like salt, while for several hours a huge convoy went safely the wrong way, before turning about, and coming back through the battle zone as if it had never happened.

We watched tight lipped as our air escort found us next morning, and practised with safety catches firmly on as we followed them through our gun sights as they zoomed across us, and let the air out of our lifebelts as it was so damned uncomfortable walking about with those things blown up under our coats. We were going southwards into the warm weather of dolphins and flying fish, of white uniforms, oiling the guns, painting out the rust on our paintwork, shining the brasswork with Bluebell, scrubbing decks, messdecks, and flats.

Once, we approached a waterspout, but stopped just short of it, listening to the roar as it sucked up the sea into the black cloud that hovered above it. There were hookers during the dog watches, hosepipe battles during scrubbing deck sessions in hot weather, and tombola on the Stoker's messdeck before supper.

Creeping up to an anchorage in fog with the echo sounder in the wheelhouse giving the depth of water, but just in case something unexpected happened and she ran aground, it would look better at a court of enquiry if the chains were manned with an experienced seaman taking soundings with a lead and line, so Leading Seaman Scargill was put in the chains, and demonstrated to all of us on the forecastle just how much notice the people up on the bridge were taking of his reports.

"By the mark ten, Sir."

The answer shouted from the Bridge. "Very good."

Scargill looked at all of us to make sure we were watching. "Stick it in your pipe, Sir!"

And from somebody up on the bridge. "Very good."

How quickly it could all change at the touch of a button.

One dark night a blip on the radar indicated something unexpected a long way ahead. Time enough to turn the convoy aside when we knew more about it, so signalling full ahead and with her crew going silently to Action Stations, the *Wellington* rapidly left her station and steamed swiftly away into the night with her white wake creaming away behind her.

Steel helmets and anti-flash gear on, all guns loaded and safety catches off, searchlight lit, but not open, watertight doors and hatches closed tight. Radar was passing the ranges, and the 4.7s were following their clocks in the darkened turrets.

Whatever it was, they had no idea of our approach. If this was a submarine, they had no chance now, our hefty 4.7s would hit with four broadsides before they could move, and the Oerlikons would make sure they could never reach their gun.

Turning slightly so that both big guns could bear, came the whispered orders. "Stand by. Open searchlights." And there in the white beam, only a button away from destruction, was a beautiful three masted sailing ship with all sails set, listing under the wind as she cut through the water.

White faces appeared along her deck, staring up at our light. She was flying no flag, no indication of who she was. Our loud hailer on the bridge began to hum as the power was switched on.

"Heave to. Stand by to receive my boarding party." It would have been suicide for them to disobey with all those guns pointing at them. As her sails came down and her speed fell away, our starboard seaboat was turned out and an armed crew from below deck went off to her.

The *Wellington* never stopped. We were experts at this game, and could lower and slip our seaboats and pick them up again while travelling at speed, and we circled that ship as our boarding party went aboard to find out who she was.

After a while, a light flickered as the Signalman in the boarding party reported back, and the tension began to ease, safety catches went on, tin hats were pushed to the back of heads, anti-flash gloves and helmets were put back into the ready use ammunition lockers.

She was Portuguese. On passage from the Azores to Lisbon with a cargo of new potatoes. New potatoes? Our long empty spud locker was sitting there useless like the open mouth of a starving man, while we had to make do with that emergency reserve called boiled rice.

It didn't take us long to drop our port seaboat as well, and in the middle of the night, between Portugal and the Azores, that beautiful schooner filled our spud locker with lovely new potatoes, and twenty odd sackfuls were stacked on our upper deck as well. We paid for them of course, and well before dawn was back in position at the head of an unsuspecting convoy. During that morning, in quiet weather, each of the four escorts were called up to come alongside, and we practised our seamanship by passing sacks of spuds across by breeches buoy. During the afternoon, after due warning that we were going to carry out some exercises, we steamed off out of the way, and dropped a single depth charge set to explode at fifty feet.

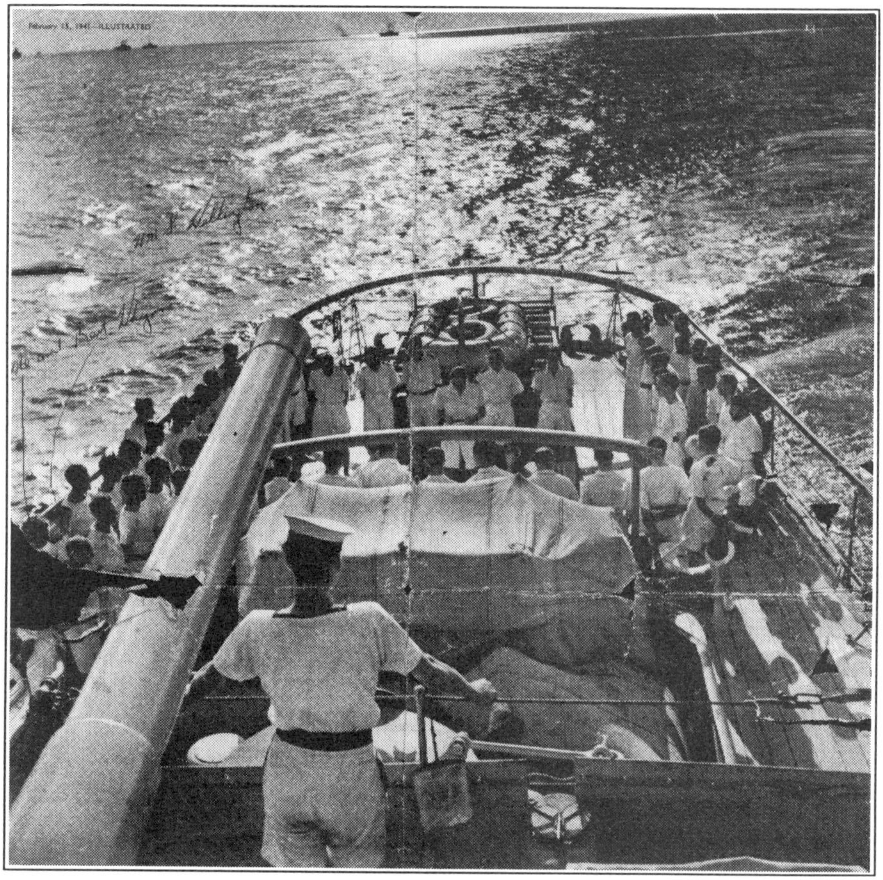

Sunday morning church.

The fish we got! They filled our seaboat twice over. Smelling like a trawler, we got back on station and called up the other escorts again, passing over buckets of fresh fish to go with the new potatoes they had. Supper that night of fish and chips was something to remember for always. We didn't know how to make batter, but Chef did. The sea was calm, and the galley was full of the smells of cooking that spread over the whole ship. With hot bread that he had baked that afternoon, even the watch on deck, who would have their supper later, sent the Bosun's Mate down for chip butties as they couldn't wait. The bridge lookouts swore they saw our Captain sitting on his seat in the corner of the bridge eating fish and chips out of a month old newspaper. As he was the one who had made it all possible, we hoped his Steward would give him a double whack.

Takoradi was our destination for this trip, and we made it just one day before Christmas. It began to look like we would have a Christmas ashore at last, the first one since we had left Training Division.

A lovely harbour opened up as we approached from seawards, and we berthed alongside the wall with enough time to get changed into spotless white suits and spend Christmas Eve ashore. It was already getting dark as we reached the first bar. It wasn't very big, and was lit by gas lamps. There was a constant sizzling and popping sound as the flies or gnats got burnt up by the mantles. We stared wide eyed at the shelf behind the counter, which was full of bottles of well known brands of whisky, so each of us had a bottle and a glass, and were soon incapable of moving any further.

Chopper turned out to be the strongest. Somehow he got me and Fred back to the harbour, but a cargo of coal had been deposited on the dockside in our way, so he said after.

A likely story! Who would be unloading a cargo of coal late on Christmas Eve? He had probably lost his way back but wouldn't admit it. Our Jaunty saw us coming aboard, decided we were no danger to anyone, and as it was Christmas Eve anyway, shook his head in despair, and looked the other way.

I woke up at quarter to five next morning lying on the upper deck alongside the funnel. Chopper and Fred were laying nearby, and we looked like coal miners who had refused to bath for a week, but the most frightening thing was the whine of the turbines and the swish of the sea. It was still dark, but I could see the smoke streaming flat away from the funnel above.

"Christ!" muttered Chopper, sitting up. "We're at sea! What

day is it?"

It was early in the morning on Christmas Day, 1943. The duty watch had taken the *Wellington* out of the harbour after a report of a submarine off Lagos.

It would be a couple of years yet before the Royal Navy would agree to let me spend Christmas ashore. Christmas 1945 would find me a Petty Officer off Okinawa in the Pacific reading a greetings telegram from Susan, but for now we were sprinkling depth charges, Christmas Day or otherwise, just like C in C Western Approaches had ordered.

We didn't find our submarine. But if he was there, I'll bet he didn't much enjoy his turkey dinner.

I tore my hand while reloading one of the throwers, and later in the sick bay watched Doc preparing to put some stitches in it. He was sitting on that same low stool from where he had carried out our short arm inspection. I saw the needle being pushed into one side of the cut, then the cut opened as the point tried to come out of the other side. As he pulled the thread tight, both holes broke through, and the needle and thread came away, and I fainted clean off. I woke up on the floor with a pillow under my head.

The doctor was there now, and they both stared down at me as if I was something one of our depth charges had brought up.

"You should have soaked his hand in hot water to soften the skin," advised the doctor.

And our sick bay Tiffy, with memories of that short arm inspection still fresh in his mind, grated, "It's not his skin that needs softening!" As he helped me up, he seemed to relent a little. "Sorry mate, but I've got to learn too".

"Meet me at tot time," I threatened him. "Instructions are expensive on Christmas Day".

My time with HMS *Wellington* was coming to an end. The war in the Atlantic seemed to be slackening, and we brought her safely up river in Freetown in March 1944, saluting the base ships *Philocoties* and *Edinburgh Castle* before coming to anchor with a precision that must have been the envy of every ship that saw her. On the order from the bridge of 'Let go', the anchor would be slipped, the boom swung out, seaboats and motorboat turned out and lowered, gangway rigged, all happening at the same time in a well rehearsed drill that took just a few minutes. Motor launches from the base ships would be waiting to come alongside with mail and orders.

On the 25th March, 1944, I waited with kit bag and hammock on the quarterdeck for the launch to take me off to King Tom Jetty en route for Kissy Barracks just outside Freetown. Promoted to Leading Seaman, there was no room for me now on HMS *Wellington*. No words of mine can describe the utter feelings of homesickness one feels on leaving a well loved ship. She had taken us as boys, and made us men, and I felt as a child felt for it's mother, or a man for his wife. She was our home, our pride, our safety. A means of venting our anger, she could smash and destroy anything we turned against. She could alter a calm sea into a vomiting nightmare. And I was saying goodbye to her. All my friends from Training Division were lining the rails holding their hands up in silent farewell as the launch bobbed away, seeing her getting smaller and smaller, trying desperately to pretend it was just splashes of sea water thrown up from the bows of the launch that flecked my manly cheeks.

I would see her twice more before her quiet retirement on the Thames, passing her there at anchor in Freetown as I sailed by on HMS *Folkstone*, going home, and they blasted *White Christmas* over the loud hailer at us as we passed, and again a few months later back home in Plymouth while I was a Petty Officer then on the Provost Staff. I recognised her masthead in the dockyard, and took my landrover and a six man patrol alongside just to satisfy a longing to feel the safety of her deck under my feet for a brief moment. Fred, Chopper and the others were still there, and they looked with envy at my landrover, while I looked with envy at their *Wellington.*

EPILOGUE

I hope I have conveyed the meaning of the love a man can have for a ship, and assure our girls that it can never vie for the love we have for them. If you should see someone throwing a kiss to a ship, it will not be to just a ship, but to a past love.

Thank you, HMS *Wellington,* we know you will silently acknowledge our salutes as we pass you by. We all owe them to you.